A 100-DAY

a Journey on the King's Road

volume one

MARILYN ELSHAHAWI

A Journey on the King's Road

Trilogy Christian Publishers A Wholly Owned Subsidiary of Trinity Broadcasting Network

2442 Michelle Drive Tustin, CA 92780

Rights Department, 2442 Michelle Drive, Tustin, CA 92780.

Trilogy Christian Publishing/TBN and colophon are trademarks of Trinity Broadcasting Network.

Cover design by Tanya Elshahawi

For information about special discounts for bulk purchases, please contact Trilogy Christian Publishing.

Trilogy Disclaimer: The views and content expressed in this book are those of the author and may not necessarily reflect the views and doctrine of Trilogy Christian Publishing or the Trinity Broadcasting Network.

Manufactured in the United States of America

10 9 8 7 6 5 4 3 2 1

Library of Congress Cataloging-in-Publication Data is available.

ISBN: 978-1-68556-979-2

E-ISBN: 978-1-68556-980-8

a Journey on the King's Road

volume one

My dear Alexandra,

I call you "Sasha." You only know me by and call me "Lola." You are still too young and too little, but someday, you will be old enough to read this book. I hope you will tell me what you think of it and also tell me about the journey you are beginning on the King's road. A world where the possibilities are endless awaits you. So, dare to go beyond the limits and allow yourself to venture into interesting places that will lead you to a deeper understanding of yourself and your King. Somewhere along the way, meet me at your various milestones, and you will be able to share your journey as you consider what you've seen and heard from me. And perhaps, you will teach me truths that I will take to heart. I will always be there as your Lola, who loves you.

Acknowledgments

Writing a book is much harder than I thought. And to you, I offer my humble gratitude and thanks. None of this would have been possible without the encouragement, help, and support of the following:

My husband and my precious children—for your love, care, understanding, and generous belief to embark on this journey with me.

Tanya Elshahawi—for sharing your gift of time and talent. I am especially blessed that my cover designer is an amazingly talented graphic designer and also my daughter.

Nancy Beauval—for that bus ride that turned into years of friendship. I am deeply grateful for your valuable support with your comments and feedback to make the book read better.

Virginia Aquino—my special thanks for making sure I cross my *t*'s.

TBN and Trilogy Christian Publishing—a very special thanks for making me a part of your TBN family. From initial contact, you welcomed my concept, my vision. Thank you for your confidence and guidance in bringing the vision to life.

All of you who helped me get there with your encouraging words, symbolic gifts of a book, a quill, and a gold pen—I very much appreciate your being there beside me even in the rough times: Carol Pisano, Deborah Daniels Andrews, Eunice Bennet, Laura Carbone, Maria Westbrook, Sheri Coleman.

Most of all, I want to thank God. I could not have done this without His inspiration, revelation, and direction.

Contents

Preface

Life is a journey. We begin our journey as we head on the King's road. It's the road that's been traveled by many. While many follow the path, many are still searching, and others may have taken the wrong turn and got lost along the way.

It is the *road* that leads to the *kingdom* that's way, way out of this world. I heard about it from my father, who then gave me his *book*. He must have loved this *book*—pages were worn, many of them marked with red-, green-, blue-, and black-colored pens. I learned about a kingdom where there's no sickness, pain, or sorrow, one with many mansions, and where streets are lined with gold, where there're gates of pearl, walls lined with jasper and precious stones, where there is no night and darkness.

I came across the pages of some of those who walked before me, even those from thousands of years ago, their personal struggles, battles, and those who tried to stop them from finding their way. There were roadblocks and detours; some got lost, but the King sent them provisions, a search party, and reinforcements to fight their battles.

Their stories stirred my mind to seek things unseen, the many things that I thought I knew and understood but that were clouded and tainted. Knowing about the King is not the same as knowing the King. As I journeyed with them, they led me to explore interesting places and gave me a new vision and strength to walk the straight path. There's so much to discover and so many possibilities!

Along the King's road is a junction that leads to many side roads. There's an unpaved path by a meadow inviting one to pause and enjoy the scent of that beautiful lily of the valley. Or to camp by a fire to rest on a dark, dark, starry night. But nothing compares to the hope and the wonder of discovering this unexplainable joy—the fullness of joy in knowing the King and finding a new meaning of who He really is.

As we connect with the generations that have gone before us, may their stories lead us to also discover new places and find new revelations about our King and what He will do for us in our very own journey.

Will you dare to go beyond the borders?

The Forbidden Tree

[...] but you shall not eat of the tree of the knowledge
of good and evil; for in the day that you eat of it,
you will surely die.

Genesis 2:17 (WEB)

It was the sixth day of creation, and we learned about the tree of the knowledge of good and evil.

Genesis 2:15–17 said the Lord God took the man and placed him in the garden of Eden to work it and watch over it. Everything was good for food, and the tree of the knowledge of good and evil was pleasing to the eyes, but it was not good for Adam and Eve to eat. If they did, they would surely die. God's command was explicit, and the consequence for disobedience by eating the fruit of this tree was clear. Why was the tree placed in the garden only for Adam to be told not to eat its fruit? So, what was the purpose of this forbidden tree?

When God created man, He created him in His image and likeness. God set man apart from the rest of His creation when He gave man the mind and the free will to choose to love and serve Him willingly or reject and rebel against Him.

God gave man everything except that one tree of the knowledge of good and evil. One particular tree! What can be so difficult with that?

13

The story of the forbidden tree and the original sin is relevant today. Adam and Eve's disobedience brought not only natural death but separation from God when they were ultimately cast out of the garden. And Adam's sinful nature was passed down to the rest of humanity.

The forbidden tree represents man's obedience—the willingness and ability to do whatever God asks. It's the choice between God and man's selfish desire. We may not always understand God's ways, but if we don't trust and obey God, we live through the consequence of rebellion.

So, sin began with the disobedience of Adam by his eating the forbidden fruit of one specific tree. It brought death and separation from God. And thousands of years later, it was ended with the obedience of Jesus Christ when He died on the cross. But this second "tree" brought death, which led to redemption, restoration, and reconciliation with God and eternal life.

The forbidden tree in the garden was not the cause of man's sinfulness but man's disobedience to God.

Today we continue to have free will. Everything is good and pleasant to the eyes, but there remains a fruit that may not be good for you and me.

What will our choice be?

Choose God!

Faith to Believe

And he believed in the LORD,
and He accounted it to him for righteousness.

Genesis 15:6 (NKJV)

We meet Abraham and Sarah in Genesis, chapter eleven. Abraham's father took his family with all their possessions and set off to Canaan, but when they got to Haran, they decided to settle there until his death. Soon after that, when Abraham was seventy-five years old, the Lord spoke to him to leave Haran, his father's family, and go to the land that God would show him. What followed was a bustle of preparation and packing for a long journey to somewhere that God would reveal along the way. Everyone dressed for the journey; the camels were loaded with all their belongings. The caravan rode through the wilderness, through sand paths, between shrubs, some thorny ones, while every now and then, the sound and cries of the goats and sheep echoed in the desert. Abraham and Sarah, with some families and servants, made this very long journey because God spoke to Abraham, and this new place was not only going to be his inheritance but also that of his son. There, God would bless him, and Abraham would become the father of many nations.

When God called Abraham, Abraham did not understand everything about His promise. And through the seasons of waiting, Abraham spent many dark nights when he could not see the fulfillment of His promise, but as he looked up to the heavens, the stars glimmered hope of the future, and with every passing day, for each step that he made on those hot desert sand, he was also reminded of the same promise (Genesis 15:5, 22:17). He did not consider that his own body, at a hundred years old, was as good as dead and that Sarah's womb was also dead.

We, too, have our own journeys. We make plans with hopes for a better future. Do we trust God to lead us out from where we are to a better place? How many of us made plans to go somewhere or do something but, somewhere along the way, got sidetracked and did not do as planned? These certain circumstances beyond our control may have caused delays or setbacks. We may have unanswered questions, and though things may seem hopeless—that sickness, that relationship, that need you have been praying for, and that impossible dream you have been hoping for—it does not matter what we are seeing; say, "Lord, let it be as You said it will be." When we say what God is saying, we speak life to our body; we speak life to our circumstance. Speak and act, believing God's promises that those things that do not exist are already there (Romans 4:17).

It may not always happen at the time when we want it, and sometimes a delay can happen, but one thing is sure—God's word never fails, and it will surely come to pass when we least expect it (Habakkuk 2:3).

Against all odds, like Abraham, don't doubt. Don't give up. Keep on believing.

Noah, the Man of Faith

Only Noah was left,
and those who were with him in the ship.

Genesis 7:23 (WEB)

Our story in Genesis, chapters five to seven, says that when Adam sinned, the ground became cursed. "Lamech named his son Noah for he said, 'May he bring us relief from our work and the painful labor of farming this ground that the Lord has cursed'" (Genesis 5:29, NLT).

Noah lived at a time when the people were so corrupt, evil, and wicked that the Lord grieved with regret and decided to destroy mankind. But God found grace with Noah. He was the only righteous, "blameless man among his contemporaries" (Genesis 6:9, HCSB). So, the Lord told Noah to build an ark because there was going to be a global flood that would destroy the earth. And Noah simply obeyed.

The neighbors must have found it strange to see Noah building the ark. Imagine the many conversations that must have happened among the townspeople: "Did you see that huge structure Noah was building?" There were speculations of his mental sanity, the mocking and the remarks of what a fool he was. He was the talk of the town as a madman who was hearing voices, the voice of his God. But Noah went about steadily building the ark according to the design God gave him.

What really went on in Noah's mind? The family he had to leave behind, his uncles, aunts, brothers, sisters, nephews, nieces, cousins, and his comfortable home. No one could recall a time of flooding, so all of Noah's extreme preparation was unheard of. Noah must have tried to tell the curious ones to repent from their wicked ways. Here's old man Noah, the farmer, now the builder and also the preacher. But no one listened.

We can learn from Noah. Noah believed not because of what he knew but *whom* he knew.

Noah was warned of something that had never happened before, but he believed God because he walked in the *fear of the Lord*. It was not the fear "of being afraid" but rather one with a sense of awe and submission. And his faith was credited to him for him to become an heir of righteousness (Hebrews 11:7).

Like Noah, who "found favor in the eyes of the LORD" (Genesis 6:8, NIV), you and I today are also saved by grace. As Paul said, "For by grace are ye saved through faith; and that not of yourselves: it is the gift of God: Not of works, lest any man should boast" (Ephesians 2:8–9, KJV).

While we are reading Noah's story, we already have some knowledge of it, but what will we do when the circumstances and lifestyle of our world happen to be as in the days of Noah? Will we have faith?

Leave Your Father's House

The LORD said to Abram: Go out from your land,
your relatives, and your father's house
to the land that I will show you.

Genesis 12:1 (HCSB)

It was a challenge for Abraham, knowing he had no children and he and Sarah were way past their childbearing years. Yet he chose to uproot himself and Sarah from their family and leave everything familiar to go to an unknown territory in response to God's call (Genesis 12). He didn't know what exactly was out there, in this so-called "promised land." He didn't have a map of the area. No statistical and economic reports on hand. The only prospect he had were the stars in the heavens and the sand in the desert.

Crossing over our mind and emotions can be so difficult that it may seem a better choice to hold onto the security of what we have. It requires a mountain of faith and believing in the promise of One greater.

The journey from the past to the future, into the unknown, is the walk of faith. The Bible says if we have faith the size of a mustard seed, we can speak to that mountain to move (Matthew 17:20).

Abraham pressed forward. He learned to see beyond what was going on in the natural. He did not focus on what he was experiencing today but believed in the supernatural—and God's promise of blessing.

When God asks us to leave everything behind, we can go through feelings of fear and insecurity. We want to see where we are going. We want to know what is out there for us. But God already knows what's ahead, not only the blessings we will receive but also our reservations. When we are willing, He gives us strength and removes our fears to see His perspective of our future. It's a huge step, but when we take the risk and make that first step, we will feel the excitement to dare and go for an adventure with Him. It will be as God said. We can focus on His words: He will never leave us or forsake us. Nothing is too hard for God, for He is the God of the impossible. His words are powerful enough to accomplish what He says. What more can we ask? It will be worth it.

Go with God. Look to the promise, for the One who made it is faithful.

Lo Debar

*And the king said, Is there not yet any of the house of
Saul, that I may shew the kindness of God unto him?*

2 Samuel 9:3a (KJV)

The battle was so intense that King Saul and his son,
Jonathan, were killed. Chaos and fear overcame the house
of Saul that David would ambush the rest of them. So, the
nurse grabbed Jonathan's five-year-old son, Mephibosheth,
as they dashed to escape, but both of them tripped, crippling
Mephibosheth. Since then, Mephibosheth had been in exile
in *Lo Debar* (2 Samuel 9:4). *Lo Debar* means "no pasture."[1]
He settled in the place of nothingness, desolation, emptiness,
fear, and lack.

Often life's chaos and uncertainty bring fear and
confusion. Fear has a way of paralyzing us that we do not
walk in freedom and in the promise. What is crippling you?

Although it was customary at that time to destroy and
eliminate anyone from the previous ruler's family for the
purpose of self-preservation and revenge, David went against
this principle. He wanted to show kindness for the sake of
his friendship and promise to Jonathan. King David not
only restored everything that belonged to Mephibosheth's

---

[1] James Strong, *New Strong's Exhaustive Concordance of the Bible*
(Nashville, TN: Thomas Nelson Publishers, 1990), s.v. "Lo Debar."

grandfather, Saul, but also made him eat at the king's table for the rest of his life. Mephibosheth was surprised and humbled by the honor that King David gave him.

We are much like Mephibosheth, and King David's grace to him is a picture of God's grace to us. No matter what we are going through, whether we have nothing, though we are rejected, shamed, or disgraced, whatever it is that is crippling us, we have become like sons and daughters of God, coheirs to His kingdom.

David sought his enemies not to revenge but to bless them.

God sees us and is able to find us in our darkest moments. He wants to take us out from the place of nothingness to the *palace* and have us feast at the King's table. Nothing can separate us from His love. He will restore everything that we lost because He cares and is faithful in His covenant.

The Spring by the Road to Shur

And the angel of the LORD found her
by a fountain of water in the wilderness,
by the fountain in the way to Shur.

Genesis 16:7 (KJV)

We meet Hagar in Genesis 16. Ten years have passed since God promised Abraham and Sarah a son, but Sarah remained barren, so she arranged surrogate motherhood through her maid Hagar. Hagar became pregnant, and tension developed between the two women. Sarah became jealous, as her worst fear of barrenness became visible. To make a bad situation worse, Hagar became prideful that she was better than Sarah, so she started to disrespect, detest, and look down on her. Sarah retaliated and treated her harshly, so Hagar ran away into the desert.

Hagar wandered through the blistering heat in the wilderness and found a spring on her way to Shur. *Shur* means "wall,"[2] and, like Hagar, we too can build an emotional wall around our hearts in our attempts to hide from yesterday's

---

[2] James Strong, *New Strong's Exhaustive Concordance of the Bible* (Nashville, TN: Thomas Nelson Publishers, 1990), s.v. "shur."

shame and pain. But through her pain, Hagar found a spring with the water that refreshes the weary and lonely.

The angel asked, "Where are you going?" And Hagar said she was running away from Sarah.

"Where are you going?"

Hagar avoided answering the question, and we are not sure where she was headed, but most likely, she was going back to Egypt, where she once lived. She was running back to her past. We, too, need to check our motives, attitudes, and behavior toward our assignments. We focus on the faults of others and take offense. We run away in hopes of changing our circumstances. But where does that lead us?

The angel told Hagar to go back and face her very difficult situation and submit to Sarah. Then the angel told her of God's great plans to bless her son and his descendants to make them a great nation—words that bring comfort and hope to a mother, and Hagar felt the angel was sent by the "God who sees" (Genesis 16:13, NIV). And in that brief moment, she had to believe that she could move beyond her past and walk with confidence and assurance into the future on the promises of God.

The "God who sees" also watches over us and intercepts us when we try to run away from our painful situation. Others may not know exactly what we're going through, but God knows. He not only provides refreshing water to renew our strength but also changes our hearts to let go of pride and submit in humility even to troublesome relationships to demonstrate His love and grace.

Hagar felt a sense of peace in that if God took care of her in the wilderness, He too would be with her to face her problems with Sarah. Hagar went back hopeful, knowing that her son could have a fresh start as one with a promised blessing from God.

God's mercy and grace are far greater than our problems. His timing is perfect for sending what we need and turning impossible situations to bring healing and reconciliation to broken relationships.

The God who sees is also the God who heals.

Now I Will Praise the Lord

Now will I praise the LORD.

Genesis 29:35 (KJV)

We meet Leah in Genesis 29. Jacob loved Rachel but was tricked into marrying Leah. It may not have been her fault, but Leah became a victim of an unhappy marriage. Leah was unwanted and unloved by her husband. But Leah longed for and desperately tried to capture his heart; still, Jacob remained detached.

But the Lord saw that Leah was hated (Genesis 29:31). The Lord also saw Leah's wounded heart, so He rewarded her with children. With the birth of her firstborn son, she felt blessed. Twice she bore more sons. She named her sons to reflect her pain and the longing in her heart with the hope that her husband would now love her. But Jacob did not.

Marriage and children did not make Jacob love Leah.

Although she continued to live in a loveless marriage, Leah came to realize that God loved her. He filled the void Jacob created in her, and so, she named her fourth son *Judah*, "praise" (Genesis 29:35).

Leah was not Jacob's choice, but this rejected and unloved wife was loved by God. In the family, Leah was the firstborn daughter and the first wife who had six sons and one daughter, and in the end, Leah was honored. If she only knew that she was laid to rest with the family ancestors when Jacob asked to be buried next to her where his parents, Isaac and Rebecca, and Abraham and Sarah, were buried (Genesis 49:29–33).

Out of man's deception and rejection of the unplanned marriage, we see God's grace to Leah. The priesthood of Levi and the line of kingship were both through Leah's sons. Through her son Judah, the nations of the world were blessed with the Savior.

Leah was not perfect, and neither are we. We can be encouraged that man can disappoint and fail us, but when we come and surrender our hearts to God with our praise, He defines and shows us our true worth. When we allow God to fill our unfulfilled desires, He is gracious to give us something greater than ourselves.

When Life Is Not Fair

"Bring her out!" Judah said. "Let her be burned to death!"

Genesis 38:24 (HCSB)

Do you keep hearing voices in your mind that things are never going to change? "There is nothing that can be done for you." "That loved one will never come back." "Your marriage was wrong, to begin with." "You'll never get to that level; you're not good enough." You see every mistake you've made. All to say, "What's the point of even trying?" But you are not alone.

The story in Genesis 38 was about a Canaanite woman named Tamar, who was married to the oldest son of Judah. He was wicked, and the Lord took him, leaving her a childless widow. According to custom, Judah arranged for his second son to marry her so that the oldest son would have an heir, but he was a wicked man too and died, leaving her childless again. Judah blamed Tamar for the deaths of his sons, so he sent her to her family with a promise of marriage to the youngest son when he was old enough. Years passed, and as she waited, she realized that Judah was not going to fulfill his obligation because the youngest son had grown, yet Judah did not make wedding arrangements.

One day, she heard about Judah going to Timnah to shear the sheep. She disguised herself as a shrine prostitute, and when Judah saw the prostitute, not knowing that it was Tamar, he asked for her services and promised to pay her with a goat. She asked for a guarantee, so he left her his seal, cord, and stick until he sent the goat.

And she became pregnant.

Not to justify what Tamar did—but the Canaanites were pagans, and the women had different values. Fornication and prostitution were acceptable rituals in their worship. Tamar suffered tragedy after tragedy, injustice from the man who had a responsibility to help her. In her desperation, Tamar was driven to fight back in her own way and exposed the unrighteousness of her accuser. A shameful and shocking story, but the Bible did not hide it.

Judah was enraged when he found out that Tamar was pregnant by a "random" man and demanded her to be burned. Before they killed her, she sent word to Judah: "The man who owns these things made me pregnant. Look closely. Whose seal and cord and walking stick are these?" (Genesis 38:25, NLT). Judah realized that she was more righteous than he because he did not fulfill his obligation and responsibility to her (Genesis 38:26). As 1 Timothy 5:8 (WEB) says, "If anyone doesn't provide for his own, and especially his own household, he has denied the faith, and is worse than an unbeliever." Judah brought her back to his home but did not sleep with her again. Both Judah and Tamar sinned because of that illicit union, but God worked all things, and their son,

Perez, became the ancestor of David and Jesus.

Are you coming to the point of desperation because of all the things that are happening in your life? Are you being blamed for some tragedy that is not your fault? Have those whom you trust turned their backs on you? Are you going to justify doing the wrong thing to get what you want, as Tamar did? God sees us. He is our defender, and He will also orchestrate everything to work for our good (Romans 8:28).

Overcoming Temptation in the Workplace

[...] how then can I do this great wickedness, and sin against God?

Genesis 39:9 (KJV)

First John 2:15-17 says we can face three areas of temptation: the lust of the flesh, the lust of the eyes, and the pride of life. Can we overcome any or all of these temptations? We look at the life of Joseph in Genesis 39:1-23.

Joseph was a slave in a foreign land to Potiphar, but he maintained his identity and worked with all his heart for the Lord, so he succeeded in everything that he did. And Potiphar was blessed because of Joseph, but Potiphar's wife was attracted to Joseph.

Joseph knew his boundaries, being fully aware of the moral code in marriage, that to violate it is against God (Genesis 39:9). He remained steadfast, but Potiphar's wife was even more determined to go after him. And so, one ordinary working day, while no one was around, she grabbed him, saying, "Come sleep with me." Joseph didn't pause or try to reason but ran quickly, leaving his robe, or tunic, in her hand.

Satan is relentless and will not give up until he finds a way to trap us. Don't rationalize—*run*!

Joseph was alone, so there was no one around to witness what happened. This same situation can happen to us. We can't flirt with temptation, believing that we are strong to fight it alone, and fall into Satan's traps.

Joseph stood for righteousness and paid a high price by being sent to prison for a crime he didn't commit. Even in his darkest times, Joseph did not question or blame God or turn away from Him. What would you and I have done or felt if we were in Joseph's position? Would we still have faith?

Joseph's story can be our guide. No man is exempt from temptation. When we are blessed by God with success, we can also expect temptation. We will be tempted in different areas of our lives, but it's the decisions and choices that can make us sin. It takes determination and disciplined steps to develop spiritual strength and stamina to gain self-control. Knowing who we are in God prepares us for anything that may arise.

> No temptation has taken you except what is common to man. God is faithful, who will not allow you to be tempted above what you are able, but will with the temptation also make the way of escape, that you may be able to endure it.
>
> 1 Corinthians 10:13 (WEB)

A Woman Named Asenath

*Pharaoh called Joseph's name Zaphenath-Paneah.
He gave him Asenath, the daughter of Potiphera
priest of On as a wife.*

Genesis 41:45 (WEB)

It all began in the capital of Egypt at the palace when the pharaoh had a dream. It was not business like usually. The pharaoh had special meetings with diviners and seers, but no one could interpret his dream. Word was given that a prisoner had the ability to interpret dreams, so Joseph was immediately called to appear before the pharaoh. And God gave Joseph the revelation to interpret his dreams.

The pharaoh was pleased with Joseph's interpretations of his dreams, so he appointed Joseph as his second-in-command to prepare the country for the coming famine. Then he arranged for Joseph to marry an Egyptian woman to show the people that Joseph, a Hebrew, had now become one of them, most likely as a political and social strategy to strengthen his choice of Joseph in the government. And Asenath, daughter of a high priest of the sun god Ra, was given to Joseph to be his wife.

Nothing much was written about Asenath in the Bible, but we can imagine all the excitement at the palace preparations for her wedding, but it was probably nothing compared to the frightening prospects of this unexpected marriage. The Egyptians did not really know much about Joseph except that he was a foreigner and a prisoner. What kind of man was he to claim fear of God yet be accused of rape? How could he have convinced the pharaoh of his claimed revelation from God that no other seasoned seer could do? How did he influence the pharaoh to appoint him to the highest position in the government? But no one dared to say no to the pharaoh.

This interracial marriage of Joseph and Asenath, the marriage of a Jew and a gentile, broke the walls of division and paved the way for peace and reconciliation to a nation and brought redemption and salvation from death and destruction to the world.

When Joseph brought his two sons to Jacob, his father, Jacob adopted them as his own, and they became part of the twelve tribes of Israel.

God always had a plan for the gentiles—even before the gospel was preached by the early church. We see how God used Asenath, a gentile, and how her children were adopted into the family of God to fulfill His plan of salvation and gave the gentiles hope for the future to become heirs to the promise (Galatians 4:5).

And still today, somewhere out there, another "Asenath" may be called to leave the confines and comfort of home for the unknown and be an instrument of God to bring radical change to the world and transform the destiny of many.

The Baby in a Basket

And Pharaoh charged all his people, saying,
Every son that is born ye shall cast into the river,
and every daughter ye shall save alive.

Exodus 1:22 (KJV)

News broke out that the pharaoh issued an order to throw all the newborn Hebrew male babies into the river. When Moses's mother could no longer hide him, she placed him in a basket and floated him on the river. Courage or faith? What was she thinking? In desperation, one can be driven to do things to the limits of faith.

The pharaoh's daughter, while bathing in the river, saw the basket, and when she opened it and saw the baby crying, she felt sorry for him. She went against her father when she took this Hebrew baby and raised him as her own son.

And Moses, as the adopted son of the pharaoh's daughter, became a member of the royal family. He was raised to be heir to the throne of Egypt and instructed in all the wisdom of the Egyptians. "He was mighty in his words and works" (Acts 7:22b, WEB).

Moses was born into slavery and was destined to die, yet the evil and deadly scheme of the enemy could not stop God's plan but only served to bring him closer to becoming the deliverer of His people.

We may never know how God will turn things around to save us from the enemy's plans of destruction. God can turn things around and make "all things work together for the good of those who love God and for those who are called according to His purpose" (Romans 8:28, WEB).

Anyone born of sin is a slave to sin, but with God's grace and mercy, He has liberated us to become heirs of His kingdom (Romans 8:15). As true sons and daughters of the King, we enter into a new relationship with God. We lose our past identity and gain new rights and privileges.

When all seems lost and the enemy thinks he's got us, God is faithful to do the impossible. He did it then. He will do it again.

He Married Zipporah, the Cushite

Moses accepted the invitation, and he settled there with him. In time, Reuel gave Moses his daughter Zipporah to be his wife.

Exodus 2:21 (NLT)

What was it like to be the wife of a legendary man like Moses?

We meet Zipporah in Exodus 2. She was the daughter of Jethro, a priest of Midian. Zipporah was a shepherdess and, together with her six sisters, roamed through the hills and the valleys, through sunny days and cold seasons, to pasture and care for their sheep.

While way beyond the border, on a deep and dark night, Moses, though raised in the best of Egypt as the adopted son of the pharaoh's daughter, dared to cross the border, leaving behind his claim to fame and power. He broke the rule of law, which he stood for, and became the enemy of the state for murder and escaped as a fugitive.

And as he walked in the wilderness, he stumbled on a well in Midian as Zipporah and her sisters came to the well to draw water for their flock. Some shepherds also came and chased them away, but Moses defended and rescued the women. They brought Moses home to meet their father. Jethro invited him to stay and later gave his daughter Zipporah to become Moses's wife. A twist of events and what may seem like a chance, an unexpected meeting brought Zipporah and Moses together and changed the course of a shepherdess's destiny.

Zipporah married a fugitive, an Egyptian murderer, but later discovered he was a Hebrew. During their forty years of marriage, she learned that he talked to this burning bush who told him to go before the most powerful man in Egypt to free his slaves.

Moses became so fully committed to his call that he failed to fulfill some of his duties at home and with the family. Did she complain? Did she really understand Moses's call or ask who this unseen "I Am" he encountered was? We don't really know, but Zipporah stepped up to fill that void. It takes a certain quality of wisdom and understanding to be a wife of a man with a high calling. Zipporah trusted and believed in her husband and the God he served. She stepped back for his priorities and stepped in for his shortcomings.

Zipporah was looked down upon by her in-laws, being a Cushite. She was different—the way she looked and talked. The way she moved. And God saw her differently, too, but not as her in-laws did, but as the faithful wife of Moses, who stood by him through the many difficulties and challenges they faced together.

Somewhere out there, God is also calling another man to climb one of the mountains. And another faithful Zipporah will be there to stand by her husband's side with love, patience, and understanding.

Tomorrow

If you refuse to let them go, behold,
I will plague all your borders with frogs.

Exodus 8:2 (WEB)

Our story in Exodus 8:1–15 began when God sent Moses to tell the pharaoh, "Let my people go so they can go and worship me" (Exodus 8:1, HCSB). But the pharaoh refused, so plagues were sent over the land of Egypt. One of them was the frogs. Frogs swarmed the Nile River and invaded the palace and every home, including the bedrooms, their beds, the kitchen, everywhere, even their ovens and food bowls. As the frogs multiplied, people also had to deal with the loud and incessant croaking of not one or a few but thousands of them through the night. Who can sleep in that setting?

So, the pharaoh called for Moses and Aaron to pray to their Lord to remove the frogs from the land. This time, he would let Moses and his people go so they could offer sacrifices to their Lord.

"When do you want me to pray so that the frogs are destroyed and only remain in the Nile River?" Moses asked.

The pharaoh answered, "Do it tomorrow" (Exodus 8:10).

Why not today? We will never know why he said, "Tomorrow." But it means one more night with the frogs.

And God could have made the frogs disappear, but God wanted them to see His great power.

Do we have a frog problem?

We may think frogs are harmless and say, "I can handle them." Are we going through dark, sleepless nights because of the noise and loud croaking that echoes through the night? Are we hoping that, by some miracle, that tormenting voice will disappear? "Maybe tomorrow it will go away." "One more day, one more night, and tomorrow I will…" After all, we look around, and we see others are going through many troubles and are struggling worse than us.

So, why choose to spend another night with the frogs?

Yes, we have a problem called *sin*. There's a constant battle within. It's not the problem of not knowing what is right but lacking the willpower to resist the carnal. Sin only leads to chaos, confusion, destruction, and death.

But healing and deliverance can be ours today. We never know what tomorrow brings, so let's not spend one more night with the frogs. We can't put off turning away from our sins before it's too late.

God's mercy and saving grace are available today.

Nowhere to Go

[...] the Israelites looked up and saw the Egyptians coming after them. Then the Israelites were terrified.

Exodus 14:10 (HCSB)

Have you ever been in a situation where things did not turn out the way you expected? You're in a very difficult place with nowhere to turn, nowhere to hide, no way of escape? The Israelites were (Exodus 14).

The pharaoh told Moses, "Leave my people—and take the rest of the Israelites with you! Go and worship the Lord as you have requested" (Exodus 12:31, NLT). The Israelites were finally leaving the place they had been calling home for 400 years and were on their way to the new land God promised them. And He led them in a roundabout way through the wilderness toward the Red Sea (Exodus 13:18). Then He told Moses to camp there next to the sea. But God hardened the pharaoh's stubborn heart even more so that he changed his mind, and his army, in their chariots, pursued the Israelites. This would be an easy victory for them but terrifying for the Israelites. They were trapped: either captured, killed, or drowned in the Red Sea.

But God was with them. He led them by a pillar of cloud by day and fire by night so that they did not get lost or make a wrong turn. So, why were they so terrified, or why did

God put them in such a dangerous place? He said, "I will be honoured upon Pharaoh, and upon all his host; that the Egyptians may know that I am the Lord" (Exodus 14:4, KJV).

And the unexpected happened when God told Moses to raise his hand over the sea: the Lord opened up a path through the water, so the people walked on dry ground through the middle of the sea as the water turned into walls on each side. When the Israelites reached the other side, God told Moses to raise his hand again, so the waters rushed back and covered the Egyptian army. With the Red Sea now closed again, there was no turning back for the Israelites.

We either have fear or faith. God is well aware of our every move. He knows every little detail of our situation. If we find ourselves trapped, maybe God brought us there for a purpose, and even in that fearful moment, God always has what's best for us and always provides a way out. God has the power to bring new directions even in the worst times of our lives. With God leading, there is only defeat for the enemy. Each step that we make takes us away from the hold of the past and brings us closer to the new things God has planned for us.

As Moses told the Israelites, "Don't be afraid. Just stand still and watch the Lord rescue you today. The Egyptians you see today will never be seen again. The Lord Himself will fight for you..." (Exodus 14:13, NLT).

And He did.

What Is It?

This evening you will know that it was the Lord who brought you out of the land of Egypt...

Exodus 16:6 (HCSB)

In Exodus 16, we follow the journey of the Israelites from Egypt to their promised land. After several days of trekking through the Sinai desert, they began to realize the difficulty and challenges of their journey and lost sight of where they came from and where they were going, but God led them this way. It was a place of testing. The landscape in the wilderness was full of danger, with the scorching heat during the day, extreme cold at night, and little or no food available. Fear and regret crept into their hearts at the looming threat of starvation, so they began to murmur and complain. They had to learn to trust God to provide for all their needs. There, they encountered God in a personal and intimate way. But they needed to let go of everything old—mindsets, habits—and embrace the new things God was doing as they transitioned to their new place.

God told Moses that He would rain bread from heaven, and they were to gather as much as they needed for the day and never to save it for the next morning. And as the blanket of dew covered the ground in the early morning, the miraculous bread of heaven rained down around the camp.

When the people saw it, they asked, "What is it?" because they did not know what it was. And so, the bread of heaven was called *manna* (Exodus 16:15, KJV).

We, too, can come to a wilderness season of testing and trying times. No one wants to go through that dry and barren land, but it may be where we are led to discover ourselves, our purpose, and our relationship with God. It's a harsh, in-between, and lonely place. It is where we feel alone, although there may be many others walking with us who are also going through tough times. In our struggle to find our true identity and as we wrestle with many deep things in our hearts, somehow, we find strength and assurance of God's presence, healing, and provision for our every need. We learn to trust Him. We also learn to fight many giants who will not only intimidate us with their shouts of threat but attempt to destroy us. But we will learn to hear God's voice and distinguish the many other tormenting voices.

Our time in the wilderness is only meant for a season. God knows all things, including every turn we make on every street corner. God may send a stranger or cause an unexpected turn of events on our behalf that we may not always realize God's working to get us through the worst time. Joy and strength when we are weary. Heart to love and forgive as we receive God's healing. Will to obey and follow God's Word and His leading.

God makes things new each day. Just as He makes the sun rise every morning, God is inviting us to arise, come and spend time with Him. The Lord wants us to start each day with Him and experience His new mercies, unfailing love, and everything we need for the day ahead. He wants to shower us with extravagant love and mercy.

The Waters at Meribah

[...] speak to the rock before their eyes, that it pour out its water. You shall bring water to them out of the rock; so you shall give the congregation and their livestock drink.

Numbers 20:8 (WEB)

The Israelites, in Numbers 20:2–13, arrived in Meribah, at the border of Canaan, their promised land. Again, there was no water. This was actually the third time they experienced a lack of water. This was an urgent need that brought fear and dread, so the congregation gathered around Moses and Aaron. What followed was an angry mob of confrontation and accusation that Moses and Aaron brought them to this place to die. Complaining and finding fault revealed their doubts and unbelief of God's promises and how quickly they forgot how God miraculously provided for their every need in the past.

Moses and Aaron sought the Lord. Two things the Lord told Moses to do: to take his rod and speak to the rock, and water would flow out for all to drink.

So, Moses and Aaron gathered the people in front of the rock. But Moses rebuked them with a claim that he and Aaron would bring the water out of the rock. Then Moses lifted up his hand and struck the rock twice with his staff so that a great amount of water came out, and the congregation and their livestock drank.

The Attitude and Behavior

The Israelites were called for something new, something better. They went this far, but their minds remained hostage to their past. They were shortsighted about where God was taking them and failed to recognize who God is.

Moses was told to speak to the rock; instead, he struck it.

The Consequence

Sadly, no one of the older generation except Caleb and Joshua, who left Egypt, made it to the promised land. And to Moses and Aaron, the Lord said, "Because you did not trust in me enough to honor me as holy in the sight of the Israelites, you will not bring this community into the land I give them" (Numbers 20:12, NIV).

We, too, can find ourselves in Meribah when we're in the valley of lack, difficulties, and temptations where our faith is challenged. Feelings of anger and frustration will surface. Our actions and attitudes will expose what is in our hearts and minds. But God looks at our faithfulness in obedience. We may not fully understand, but He knows what's best for us, and His ways are higher than ours.

Psalm 95:8 says not to harden our hearts as they did in Meribah.

God didn't take us this far to fail. But we can't strike if we are told to speak. We can't keep looking back, but with the few steps we've gone, we are to continue to press on until the breakthrough. Let us look and reach beyond where we are now. God has great things for us. They're just ahead, and with God, we will make it through.

When Your Donkey Talks

Then the Lord opened the donkey's mouth...

Numbers 22:28 (HCSB)

Numbers 22 gives us an interesting insight into a king who wants to curse God's people, a sorcerer named Balaam, and a talking donkey.

Balaam was on his way to meet the king of Moab. He was hired to curse the Israelites. He knew that these people were blessed, and he could not curse them (Numbers 22:12), but the reward money was too good to pass up. So, early in the morning, Balaam, all dressed for this journey, saddled his donkey to meet the king. With one hand pulling the rope on the donkey and the other with his rod, Balaam and his donkey strode along the narrow path between the vineyards.

God sent an angel with a sword to block him, but only the donkey saw the angel, so the donkey tried to avoid the angel and went into the field. Balaam struck the donkey to turn her back to the path. After he struck the donkey for the third time, the angel stood in such a narrow place that it was impossible for the donkey to turn in any direction. So, the donkey lay down, and Balaam became so angry he struck the donkey again. The donkey was trapped between the angel and his angry master. But the donkey knew better than to

59

stand against an angel with a sword in hand.

Strangely, the donkey spoke and asked, "What have I done to you that you struck me three times?" (Numbers 22:28, WEB). Yet Balaam was oblivious to what was happening around him. He did not even wonder how he could be engaging in a conversation with the donkey. And the donkey said to Balaam, "Am I not your donkey, on which you have ridden all your life long until today? Was I ever in the habit of doing so to you?" (Numbers 22:30, WEB).

God used the donkey to expose what was hidden in Balaam's heart. The donkey served his master in obedience and loyalty but chose to obey her Creator. Although struck and threatened, the donkey took it all in humility to save Balaam's life. "God chose the foolish things of the world that he might put to shame those who are wise. God chose the weak things of the world that he might put to shame the things that are strong" (1 Corinthians 1:27, WEB).

We may be faced with choices that draw a very fine line between good and evil, but it is only when our hearts are right with God that we are able to see the truth. We may think our ways are good, but the Lord sees our intentions (Proverbs 16:2).

Let us watch for unusual things that may happen around us. They may have some prophetic significance. When we can't get what we want, or when things do not go the way we want, it may actually be the Lord's divine interruption. And if we find that our path is blocked for some unknown reason, maybe God is pointing us in another direction.

Beyond the Power of Words

I called you to curse my enemies, and, behold,
you have altogether blessed them these three times.

Numbers 24:10 (WEB)

Numbers 22–25 tells us that the Israelites were camped by the land of Moab on their way to Canaan. Politically, the Amorites, Bashan, Moab, and Midian were against each other for many generations, but they banded together under the leadership of Balak against Israel. He hired a sorcerer named Balaam to curse and ultimately defeat them.

Balak sent messengers not to let anything stop him from going because he was willing to pay Balaam whatever price he wanted. Balaam asked God, but God forbade him, so he refused the offer. But Balak was persistent and understood the persuasive powers of money, so he raised the reward. And for the right price, Balaam agreed. The devil will try to find man's every weakness and will take advantage of that weakness.

Balak and Balaam both knew that there is power in our words. We either bless or curse; we speak life or death (Proverbs 18:21). So, Balak took Balaam to the high places of Baal for a good view of the people so Balaam could curse them. After several attempts to curse the Israelites, Balaam could only speak blessings over Israel and cursed the enemies. Now Balak became very angry, so he ordered

Balaam to go home.

We can learn from Balaam that "an undeserved curse will be powerless to harm you" (Proverbs 26:2, TPT). But Balaam knew their weakness could cause their own downfall. So before he left, he told the kings what to do.

And so, the kings of Moab and Midian arranged a feast in honor of their idol god. And the women invited the men to attend the sacrifice to their gods. The men participated in the feast and rituals and had sex with the women. As a result, a plague came upon the camp, and 24,000 died (Numbers 31:16).

The seduction and death of 24,000 men were from the malicious advice of one man who knew their weakness. This story still serves to warn us today until the end times as written in the book of Revelation 2:14 (WEB),

But I have a few things against you, because you have there some who hold the teaching of Balaam, who taught Balak to throw a stumbling block before the children of Israel, to eat things sacrificed to idols, and to commit sexual immorality.

Satan works the same way: where he cannot curse God's people, he finds their weaknesses that lead to the doors of idolatry and sexual sins.

Speaking words of truth is not enough when tainted with words that lead to sin. When we are faced with a choice, we need to ask, "What is my motive?"

God sees and knows what's in our hearts.

The Man Who Asked for a Mountain

[...] except Caleb the son of Jephunneh; he shall see it,
and to him and his children I am giving the land on
which he walked, because he wholly followed the Lord.

Deuteronomy 1:36 (NKJV)

We meet Caleb in Numbers 32:12. He was called the son of Jephunneh, a Kenizzite, so he was not an Israelite by birth. In Genesis 15:19, the Kenizzites were listed as one of the nations that God told Abraham were to be driven out. Yet Caleb, the Kenizzite, had a heart for God that he was chosen to represent the tribe of Judah along with eleven other tribes that Moses sent for a covert mission to Canaan.

Caleb and the other spies explored the land, and after forty days, they reported that the land was indeed flowing with milk and honey, but ten of the spies said the people who lived there were tall and too strong for them to conquer. Only Caleb and Joshua had a different perspective and stood against the report of the other spies.

Caleb trusted in the promise of God that, despite the people who occupied the land, God would bring them into this land (Numbers 14:8). Caleb's boldness and conviction made him refuse to be influenced by the negativity of those around him. He silenced the opposition and told them that they should go and take the land because they were well able to conquer it (Numbers 13:30).

And God rewarded his faith. He said, "But my servant Caleb, because he had another spirit with him, and hath followed me fully, him will I bring into the land whereinto he went; and his seed shall possess it" (Numbers 14:24, KJV).

Caleb asked for Hebron, the mountain that was inhabited by hostile giants. Forty years of going around that wilderness did not discourage him. Although Caleb had grown older at eighty-five years old, he told Joshua he did not feel any weaker. In fact, he felt as strong as he was the day Moses sent him out and was willing and ready to fight for his inheritance (Joshua 14:11).

Let us not also allow the past to hold us back from advancing into the promise of God. Refuse to be influenced by the naysayers. If we are in a place where we feel insecure because we see that everyone seems to be better than us— they are more educated, they are more successful—we should stop! Caleb was among the least from the tribe of Judah, yet he focused on who he was in God. He persevered, held onto God's promises despite setbacks and obstacles, and finished strong.

Our dream may seem like a mountain when we focus on our physical strength and ability to climb to the top, but God knows everything, and He sees our every misstep. He knows we're tired, but He will see that we make it through. First, He removes our fear for us to face the giants along the way.

The way we handle life's setbacks and disappointments could be our legacy to those around us. We, too, can ask for a mountain with the hope that the latter years will be greater than anything that we have ever experienced.

When Weakness Is Not Defeated

*Remember what Amalek did to you
by the way as you came out of Egypt.*

Deuteronomy 25:17 (WEB)

It all began while the Israelites were in the wilderness. The Amalekites were powerful and brutal nomads who attacked them from behind, targeting the weak and stragglers (Deuteronomy 25:17–18). And years later, in 1 Samuel 15, King Saul from the tribe of Benjamin was given a command to destroy the Amalekites, but he spared the Amalekite leader, King Agag.

Since then and for many generations, the descendants of the Amalekites continued to attack the Jews. This long-standing battle between the Amalekites and the Jews could have ended if Saul did not spare King Agag. King Saul paid a high price for such disobedience with his crown and the kingship given to David.

Generations later, in the book of Esther, Haman, a descendant of King Agag, who was prime minister of the Persian king, plotted to destroy all the Jews in the land. But Mordecai and Esther, who were also descendants of King

Saul, fought to stop Haman's evil plot.

Out of the disobedience of one man, God was able to raise a generation to stand in the gap and save the rest from total destruction.

The path that we walk, the circumstances that we deal with, the things that we wrestle with, the questions that we ask, and the things that are tied to the world may be inclinations that we inherited from our ancestral line. And our weakness can lead to sin. Having weakness is not what matters. It is how we deal with and overcome our weaknesses.

No matter how small the problem, unless it is dealt with, it can come back stronger and more destructive. But we are not meant to use that weakness as an excuse for not reaching our God-given destiny.

We can overcome our weaknesses when we have the word of God in our hearts.

> How can a young man keep his way pure? By living according to your word. With my whole heart, I have sought you. Don't let me wander from your commandments. I have hidden your word in my heart, that I might not sin against you.
>
> Psalm 119:9–11 (WEB)

With God, we can resist and overcome our every weakness because the "Lord is faithful, who will establish you and guard you from the evil one" (2 Thessalonians 3:3, WEB).

And so we say, "I can do all things through Christ, who strengthens me" (Philippians 4:13, WEB).

Rahab's Faith

[...] tie this line of scarlet thread in the window
which you used to let us down. Gather to yourself into
the house your father, your mother, your brothers,
and all your father's household.

Joshua 2:18 (WEB)

We meet Rahab, a Canaanite prostitute who lived in Jericho in Joshua 2. Now, Joshua and his army were encamped by the Jordan valley, ready to cross through Jericho on their way to the promised land. But Jericho was a fortified city, so Joshua decided to send spies before marching on to battle.

It was getting late in the afternoon, and the city gates would soon be closed. Rahab's house was by the border of Jericho and frequented by men, so the spies went there to hide. Rahab sensed that these men were strangers, but she also remembered what she had heard of how God had given them the land that brought great fear among her people. She heard how God dried up the water for them to cross through the Red Sea and how they defeated and destroyed many mighty giants in battle. Rahab believed in their God, not from a personal encounter but indirectly through the testimonies she heard.

The king of Jericho was told of the spies, so he sent soldiers to Rahab's place. Rahab lied to the authorities that the men had just left, directing the soldiers opposite to where they went. Rahab went back to the roof where she hid the spies under the stalks of flax. She came to believe in the God of the spies when she said, "For the Lord your God, he is God in heaven above, and in earth beneath" (Joshua 2:11, KJV). She believed that they would soon conquer the land, so she made an agreement to spare her life and the lives of her family when they came back to take the land. The spies agreed on the condition that she would keep their secret and if she kept her family inside the house and tied a red cord by the window as a sign.

Rahab may have made many bad choices in her life, including her having been a prostitute, but she demonstrated her faith in God when she risked her life and chose to step into her future by aligning with the God of Israel. Rahab had faith that produced good works (James 2:25). Eventually, she was no longer known as a prostitute but as a woman of faith in Hebrews 11.

In man's eyes, Rahab was a sinner, but we don't really know her heart. But God did. God knows our every thought and motive.

We, too, can make many choices in our lives that give us a reputation we can't be proud of. But God sees our hearts. All we need is faith that we, too, can come to the saving grace of God.

Gilgal

The Lord then said to Joshua,
"Today I have rolled away the disgrace of Egypt from
you." Therefore, that place is called Gilgal to this day.

Joshua 5:9 (HCSB)

A younger generation, born in the wilderness, was not circumcised according to the custom, and as they were about to enter their promised land, God told Joshua to take flint knives and circumcise them. They camped at Gilgal, right by the border of Jericho (Joshua 4:19). From a military standpoint, this was risky and dangerous, as all the men of the fighting age were quite incapable of fighting for several days until they healed. If the enemy were to attack them, it would mean total destruction, yet beyond reasonable wisdom, they were willing to risk everything and chose to trust and obey God.

Why did God instruct them to pause and be circumcised in Gilgal, where they would be at their weakest and most vulnerable, surrounded by the stronger enemy?

Gilgal was the place where God rolled away the shame and disgrace of Egypt, the memories, and the "slave" mindset. God wanted them circumcised not only in the physical but also in their hearts. They needed to separate themselves from their past and to be separated unto God, no longer as slaves, but as children of God who had a promise of an inheritance in a land flowing with milk and honey.

This generation was raised up in unbelief, but they had a call to fulfill what the previous generation had failed to do. They could not advance into the fullest potential of God's call and promise until their hearts were healed and in the right place of seeing themselves as God saw them.

We, too, have a promise of blessing. We may not have gone this way before, but many who went before us failed. We cannot be hasty in blaming others when we feel as if a sharp flint knife has just cut us through, and the pain is unbearable. Our success in advancing to our promise hinges on surrendering and letting go of our past. We must allow God to take us to Gilgal and circumcise our hearts. His way is better than ours.

Gilgal is the first stop to close a chapter, but it is also the first step toward a new beginning. It marks a new season in our journey.

Let's walk hand in hand with God for an exciting adventure in our future.

Your Walls Will Come Down

Now Jericho was strongly fortified because of the Israelites—no one leaving or entering. The Lord said to Joshua, "Look, I have handed Jericho, its king, and its fighting men over to you."

Joshua 6:1–2 (HCSB)

The story in Joshua 6 is a lesson of courage that when God tells us to do something and we move forward in faith, He removes impossible barriers to give us victory.

After forty years of wandering in the wilderness, finally, the Israelites were crossing over the Jordan River onto their promised land. Their point of entry was the military stronghold of the Canaanites in the city of Jericho, a city surrounded by thick and high walls, so invading this fortified city would not only be difficult but cause much damage and loss to the invaders.

The Lord told Joshua, "March around the city with all the soldiers. Circle the city once for the next six days. Then have seven priests carry seven trumpets in front of the sacred Chest of the Covenant. On the seventh day, circle the city seven times while the priests blow the trumpets. When you hear the sound of the prolonged horn, let the people give a mighty shout. The city walls will fall down; then have the people advance and go in" (Joshua 6:3–5, paraphrased).

This military strategy was bizarre, yet Joshua followed God's instructions to the letter. God already told him they would conquer Jericho the moment they crossed the Jordan River. Although Joshua was confident, his challenge may have been telling the people about this strange strategy. Nothing made sense, but Joshua instructed his army: "Don't talk or say a word until I say, 'Shout.' Then shout" (Joshua 6:10, paraphrased). And as they did, the walls came down.

Did you ever wonder why they were told to march in silence? Looking back at the time when the Israelites were in the desert when food supply was running out, we can see the people became impatient and spoke against God and against Moses (Numbers 21:4–5). God showed them many miracles, but the wilderness journey was characterized by an attitude of grumbling and murmuring against God. Many of those who left Egypt did not make it and did not see the fulfillment of their promise. This time, they did not complain, murmur, or grumble, not even whisper, but they pressed forward in silence as told, and the walls came down.

We, too, have our battles to conquer with impossible walls of physical infirmity or sickness, walls of division in marital or family relationships, financial struggles, and many other issues. Hear what God says. We may not understand God's strategies, especially when they seem ridiculous or illogical, but we can learn from Joshua to move in faith. God brought us through in the past; He can do it again. So, stand in faith and watch those walls come down.

Sun, Stand Still

*Sun, stand still on Gibeon! You, moon,
stop in the valley of Aijalon!*

Joshua 10:12 (WEB)

Gibeon was a large royal city with strong fighting men, but the Gibeonites lied and deceived Joshua into making a peace treaty with them. When the Amorites heard about this treaty, five Amorite kings joined forces to attack Gibeon. The Amorites were tall and fierce warriors from the hill country, so the Gibeonites appealed to Joshua for help. Despite the deception, Joshua honored the agreement he made with the Gibeonites.

While Joshua and his army marched all night, the Lord told Joshua not to be afraid because not one of them would be able to stand against him (Joshua 10:8). They took them by surprise as the Lord threw the Amorites into confusion. Many fled, but Joshua pursued them. Then the Lord sent large hailstones, and many of the Amorites died from the hail more than the swords of Joshua's army. The battle was raging, and the sun was quickly sinking, but Joshua was determined to get this done and over with.

And Joshua dared to ask for a bigger miracle to give him more time and extend the day.

And the sun stood still, and the moon stopped until they had complete victory before darkness (Joshua 10:13). No man had ever prayed as boldly as Joshua commanded the forces of nature. "There has been no day like it before or since, when the Lord listened to the voice of a man" (Joshua 10:14, HCSB).

We, too, may have an Amorite, a fierce enemy who is coming against us first and then—our loved ones. God is faithful to fulfill His every word. We can ask boldly for the impossible because our victory is in the Lord our God, who goes with us and fights our battles. He never sends us to fight alone. He goes ahead and is right beside us so that no one and nothing, not even the forces of nature, can delay or stop us. And so we say, "The Lord is my helper. I will not fear. What can man do to me?" (Hebrews 13:6, WEB).

God did it for Joshua. He will do it again for you and me.

Unfruitful in the City of Palm Trees

So the waters were healed to this day,
according to Elisha's word which he spoke.

2 Kings 2:22 (WEB)

Jericho was called the "city of palm trees" (Deuteronomy 34:3), yet the men asked Elisha for help because, in spite of the city's good location, the water was bad and the land unfruitful (2 Kings 2:19). This may have begun hundreds of years prior when Joshua invoked a curse on anyone who would rebuild this city (Joshua 6:26). Since then, although the place looked nice and beautiful on the outside, the land was barren and the water was polluted, causing much sickness, including miscarriages among women. So, Elisha asked them to bring him a new bowl and put salt in it. Then Elisha went out to the spring of water and threw salt in it (2 Kings 2:20–21, WEB).

We all experience ups and downs at varying times in life, but a persistent hardship, lack, misfortune, or trouble may be an indicator of a curse. Like Jericho, our prospects on the outside may look good, but the reality is our challenges are causing us to expend much of our time and strength trying to gain headway. We strive to regain our health, restore our finances, and improve our circumstances, yet we continually experience frustration, defeat, or failure. We try to do something different and hope to succeed. We're almost at the finish line, but things suddenly fall through, and we can't explain why.

We do not have to let the curse define us and live in that cycle of barrenness. The curse is real, and it can be broken, but the root of the problem must be dealt with in the spiritual connection.

Three Things That Elisha Needed

Salt. The Bible references salt metaphorically for usefulness and purification. Salt represents the presence of God in a believer's life and the power of God to purify man's sinful nature.

New bowl. A clean vessel keeps the salt pure and free from contamination.

The source of the problem. Elisha did not waste his time examining the symptoms and the outward manifestation of the problem.

Salt, as the presence of God in a believer's life, makes us the vessels in the hand of the Lord. Our *renewal* in the Spirit is the first step to healing and deliverance. Once our bowl is renewed, then the salt can be poured into the bitter waters of our lives and change the flow from the source to sweet water.

And we know that Jericho's healing was complete to this day as Elisha spoke (2 Kings 2:22).

Let us come before the Lord for our freedom and healing to end barrenness. We, too, can do the symbolic act of faith and reverse the curse that has kept us from advancing into our promised blessing. Receive your healing today.

The Jar Will Not Become Empty

So there was food every day for Elijah
and for the woman and her family.

1 Kings 17:15 (NIV)

There was nowhere to go, no one to run to for help, and the only thing this widow could do was face the painful reality of dying at the height of the famine. Having a scoop of flour and some oil, the widow was gathering wood to bake bread for their last meal. As heartbreaking as her situation may be, she had no idea of the wonderful things that God had planned for her.

There was a famine in the land, as we read in 1 Kings 17:7–16. Somewhere in another city, God told Elijah to go to Zarephath because He commanded a widow to provide food for him. When Elijah saw the widow, he asked her to give him a cup of water. And as she was going to get it, he asked her for a piece of bread too.

Famine and death were the only realities in her world. She wondered, *I can't believe this man is asking me for water and food.* So, she said, "As the Lord your God lives, I only have about a small scoop of flour and some oil. I'm picking up some firewood to cook our last meal so my son and I can eat our last meal and die" (1 Kings 17:12, paraphrased). We don't really know what she believed or what and if she heard from God about Elijah.

"Don't worry. Go ahead and make the cake but give me the first portion. Then, you can have the rest for yourself and for your son," Elijah replied.

Then Elijah said, "The bin of flour shall not be used up, nor shall the jar of oil run dry, until the day the Lord sends rain on the earth" (1 Kings 17:13–14, NKJV).

Beyond the limitations of the boundaries of our realities, let us look with the eyes of faith at the promises for the blessings of God.

God provided supernaturally to take care of His own and those who don't know Him. Elijah was sent not to the rich and great men of wealth and honor but to the lowly and poor widow. Elijah's faith and obedience led him to go somewhere as a foreigner and ask for help from the unlikely, poor, and desperate. The widow had the heart to honor God with everything she had as an act of surrendering her life and her son's life to the God of miracles though she had not known Him before.

God works in mysterious ways, for "God chose the weak things of the world that he might put to shame the things that are strong" (1 Corinthians 1:27, WEB).

No matter how little or insignificant the thing in our hands is, when we offer it to God, He blesses and multiplies it beyond our understanding. He is our provider, and He will do great and mighty things that will astonish those around us when we give Him the best of what we have.

The Marriage and Covenant of Ahab

But there was none like unto Ahab,
which did sell himself to work wickedness in the sight
of the Lord, whom Jezebel his wife stirred up.

1 Kings 21:25 (KJV)

Ahab married Princess Jezebel, daughter of the king of Sidon (1 Kings 16:31), most likely for political reasons, and together they ruled the northern Kingdom of Israel. After their marriage, Jezebel became actively involved in the leadership. She introduced the worship of Baal and convinced Ahab to build a temple for Baal. Ahab became notorious as an evil king because he devoted himself to worshiping Baal because his wife, Jezebel, influenced and persuaded him.

During the course of their reign, Ahab wanted a piece of land that belonged to Naboth, but Naboth refused to sell his ancestral land. Ahab sulked, not being able to get his way, but Jezebel issued an order under the king's name to have Naboth killed, then seized his vineyard.

Ahab was a weak husband who did not assert his conviction of the lordship of the God of Israel. He loved and respected his wife, and Jezebel took that as an upper hand to turn him against God. When Ahab married Jezebel, he created an unholy alliance. He abandoned his God to worship Baal, the god of Jezebel.

Like Ahab, many who follow the Jezebel doctrine become blinded to God's Word. They forsake God and turn their devotion to other gods or things. They cannot see the deception but believe in lies that lead to death and destruction. As it is written: "Behold, you trust in lying words that can't profit. Will you steal, murder, commit adultery, swear falsely, burn incense to Baal, and walk after other gods that you have not known" (Jeremiah 7:8–9, WEB).

We can ask God to open our eyes so that we are not in agreement with someone who is in rebellion. That person can be seductive and persuasive to lead us away from the truth, and slowly, we will find justification to do many inappropriate things. All great things start with something small, so let's be aware that we are not seduced and deceived into clinging to a covenant with the world. We can be blinded because things are not always as they seem and what is wrong becomes right and what is right becomes wrong. Our action or inaction will significantly impact and alter the course of our life.

Victory in Mount Carmel

How long will you waver between the two sides?
If Yahweh is God, follow him;
but if Baal, then follow him.

1 Kings 18:21 (WEB)

We meet Elijah, a man with a sense of mystery because nothing much was written about him other than that he was a Tishbite, a man who had zeal (1 Kings 19:14) and boldness for God yet fled and went into hiding because Jezebel was determined to kill him and all the other prophets of God.

Our story is in 1 Kings 18 and 19. It was the third year of drought in the land. Elijah went through many hard times, but the Lord provided for his needs. Then the Lord God commanded Elijah to challenge King Ahab to gather Jezebel's prophets of Baal and Asherah to meet at Mount Carmel. King Ahab and all of Israel came to witness this confrontation. Both Elijah and the priests of Baal built an altar for each of their gods, and the god who answered with fire to consume the wood would be acknowledged as the true God. The priests of Baal could not get Baal to respond, but at Elijah's prayer, fire came down from heaven and consumed his sacrifice. Elijah then had the priests executed and went to the top of Mount Carmel.

There he prayed seven times until the Lord brought a downpour that ended the three-year drought—a dramatic and powerful demonstration of almighty God to send both fire and rain on a day.

All these astonishing miracles on Mount Carmel were great victories for Elijah and for the Lord. Elijah expected idol worship to end and the nation to repent and worship God, but he was mistaken. This challenge was meant to be a battle between God and Baal, but Jezebel made it personal between her and Elijah. Jezebel's heart remained hard. In anger, she threatened and vowed to kill Elijah, so he fled to the wilderness. He became so exhausted and depressed he told God he wanted to die. This prophet, who prayed for fire and rain that proved the power of the living God, with one threat from Jezebel, fled for his life. How could this happen? How soon could he have forgotten the Mount Carmel experience?

We can be passionate about something but feel frustrated when, after all we've done, we see no positive change in our situation. Discouraged, we cry out to God, saying, "I've done my best, but I'm fighting a losing battle. Enough, Lord."

Let's guard our hearts and our passion because our strongest conviction can become our weakest point. Look what happened to Elijah. Although he had zeal, he became so discouraged when things didn't turn out as expected. The Lord still had great work for Elijah, but he gave up, and his heart was no longer there. We can't blame ourselves as a failure when, after all we've done, in spite of our best effort, the world rejects us. No matter what happens, God is bigger than anything, and He can use our failure for our good and His glory. No one and nothing can keep God's perfect plan from advancing.

When You Ask for Something Difficult

Elisha picked up the mantle that had fallen off Elijah.

2 Kings 2:13 (HCSB)

Elisha was the son of a wealthy landowner who left the family business to go full-time in the prophetic ministry and was trained by the prophet Elijah. We don't hear much about Elisha during his years of training, but we read in 2 Kings 2:1–25 about how the time has come for Elijah to pass the baton to his successor. While Elijah needed to finish his last assignments in Gilgal, Bethel, Jericho, and Jordan, Elisha stayed close to his mentor, and so the two of them went together. Elijah asked, "What do you want me to do for you before I go?"

Elisha wanted a "double portion" of what this master prophet had.

Elijah replied, "You have asked a hard thing, yet if you see me when I am taken from you, it will be so for you but if not, it will not be so" (2 Kings 2:10, WEB). And as they continued walking and talking, a chariot with horses of fire suddenly appeared, and Elijah went up into heaven by a whirlwind—an awesome display of supernatural power.

The very same prophet who called down fire from heaven was now taken up to heaven by fire. Then, Elijah's mantle fell onto the ground. When Elisha saw this, he tore his clothes into two and picked up the mantle.

Thousands of years ago, Elisha dared to ask for a hard thing. Not everyone is called to be a prophet to the nation, but God can call us in other areas. What has God called you to do? Are we willing to do and ask as Elisha did?

Elijah gave Elisha a condition of granting his request if Elisha witnessed his translation.

Elisha went beyond what he saw. Elisha tore his clothes. We must be willing to let go of our old identity. We cannot change the past, but we can make changes that will affect our future and go forward with God.

The mantle was not just handed to Elisha. He had to go after what he asked for. Having the authority of a given position also comes with many challenges, like opposition and rejection that come along with that position. We cannot only look at the benefit and rewards of the gift, but we must be willing to accept the challenges and difficulties that come with that gift.

The places we visit along the way represent personal temptation, tests, or struggles that become our very own testimony of the grace and mercy of God. But we can't limit God's power and ability. Elisha asked for a difficult thing. We, too, can simply ask as Matthew 7:7 (KJV) says, "Ask, and it will be given to you..."

The Shunammite Woman

Let's set a bed, a table, a chair, and a lamp stand for him there. When he comes to us, he can stay there.

2 Kings 4:10 (WEB)

The story in 2 Kings 4:8–17 was of an unnamed woman who was simply described as the woman from Shunem. She was wealthy and married but childless. One day, Elisha, the prophet, and his servant Gehazi, came to town, and the woman knew that Elisha was a man of God, so she convinced her husband to build a room for them to stay in each time they were in town. Elisha wanted to do something in exchange for her hospitality. But she simply thanked him, giving the impression of contentment. Gehazi mentioned that she was childless and her husband was old.

Society and culture at that time placed importance on having children, and barrenness brought shame and emotional anguish. Often, it was perceived that a woman's inability to have children was a symbol of withholding the blessing from God. Some considered it a punishment and even a curse. Unlike modern times, there was no prescribed treatment other than God's miracle.

So, Elisha told her, "At this season, when the time comes around, you will embrace a son." Immediately, she cried, "No, my lord, you man of God, do not lie to your servant"

(2 Kings 4:16, WEB).

The promise of a son was an answer to the unspoken longing in her heart, and it removed her shame of barrenness. She may have lost hope and stopped believing, but now God remembered her prayers.

And today, that woman could be you and me. Have you ever had a dream like her? For instance, there is someone who is single, and you have a desire to be married. Or someone who is childless and desires to have a child. Someone who is married and desires to have a better relationship with their spouse. Someone who desires for a rebellious child to come home. Some may want to change jobs. The list can go on. We pray for our dream, but it has been so long that we can't speak of it anymore. We have our moments of hope and disappointment.

What the Shunammite woman did for Elisha and his servant was her act of offering to God without expectation of something in return. And God honored her willing heart and gave her the desires of her heart. And as Elisha spoke, the woman became pregnant and had a son.

Some of us may have given up on our prayers long ago. But God sees the longing in our hearts and the unfulfilled dreams that we buried deep inside. God wants to heal us, too, so we can dream again. So, "delight thyself also in the Lord: and he shall give thee the desires of thine heart" (Psalm 37:4, KJV). And like the Shunammite woman, let the Word of God be our promise.

The Servant Girl's Faith

*If only my master were with the prophet who is in
Samaria! For he would heal him of his leprosy.*

2 Kings 5:3 (NKJV)

In 2 Kings 5:1–19, we meet a young girl who was taken
away from her home and brought back as a slave to serve
the wife of the commander of the Syrian army. The fear and
anger of this unnamed girl forced to serve her captors while
her family grieved is an experience that no parent or child
would ever want.

The commander of the Syrian army, named Naaman, was
a brave warrior, a great and highly regarded man, but he had
the incurable disease, leprosy. The servant girl talked to her
mistress, "If he would only go to see the prophet Elisha in
Samaria, he would be healed." What can any man do to cure
an incurable disease? Perhaps out of desperation, this high-
ranking official listened to the servant girl's suggestion. So,
Naaman and his men, with their horses and chariots, took off
to see Elisha. When they arrived, Naaman was disappointed
that Elisha didn't see him. He sent word through his servant
that Naaman should go to the Jordan River and wash himself
seven times. Naaman left offended and furious but later,
reluctantly, did as he was told, and he was healed!

Did the servant girl ever have second thoughts or fear? What if Naaman will not get healed? What would the consequence be for her if the journey failed? And what would have happened to Naaman if the servant girl had the attitude of, "you deserve it because of what you did to me" or "it's none of my business and best to keep quiet"? She could have said, "I'm a nobody; who would listen to me?" Instead, with compassion and boldness, she shared her faith in the miraculous power of the living God whom she knew.

And God was able to use this unnamed girl to bring salvation, healing, and deliverance, not only to one man but to his household and, probably, many others who were under his command.

And today, we may find ourselves in a strange and foreign land, among the least likely, but God may have sent us there even with misgivings as reluctant missionaries to win the hearts and souls of many to the saving grace of God. We don't have to speak eloquently like an evangelist, but God sees everything. And He will empower us to speak words that bring deeper healing not only in the physical but also healing from arrogance and pride as Naaman.

Let's not put ourselves in a position where we say, "I wish I spoke up," but ask God to give us the courage and be a blessing to share our faith in God's saving grace to the hopeless and dying.

The God Who Restores

The woman arose, and did according to the man
of God's word. She went with her household,
and lived in the land of the Philistines for seven years.

2 Kings 8:2 (WEB)

Have you ever been told, "We were just talking about you?"

In 2 Kings 8:1–6, we read about a dismal situation where the nation was going to be hit with a seven-year famine. Elisha, the prophet, went to warn the Shunammite woman whose son he had restored to life. He told this unnamed woman to leave and move to a faraway land because of the coming famine. The Shunammite woman who owned farmlands and a home did not wrestle with Elisha's words but packed up, uprooted her family, and sought refuge in the foreign land of the Philistines (an enemy territory).

And seven years later, when the famine ended, she came home only to find that her house and land had been seized by the king. If God spared her life, why did He allow her house and land to be taken away from her? But she went to the king to appeal for her house and land. And as she entered the king's court, Gehazi, Elisha's assistant, just happened to be talking to the king about the miracle that Elisha did in bringing the Shunammite's dead son back to life. Was this a coincidence?

And so, the King became curious and attentive to the woman's story. The king was so impressed that he assigned an official to her case and said, "Restore all that was hers, and all the fruits of the field since the day that she left the land, even until now" (2 Kings 8:6, WEB).

The God who cares is also the God who restores. The woman was not only spared from death in time of famine but received restoration of her house and land. And beyond her expectation, she received restitution for all the income that she lost over the years.

May this woman's story, with the many twists and turns of her life, encourage us that the God who cared for her yesterday is the same God who cares for you and me today and will be for our children and the succeeding generations to come.

And today, devastating things can happen, beyond our control, that threaten us to lose everything. Difficult situations, whether in health, marital or family relationships, or finances—some may be more traumatic. But no matter how gloomy or hopeless the situation may be, did God not say, "Behold, I am the Lord, the God of all flesh. Is anything too hard for me" (Jeremiah 32:27, KJV)? With God, things do not simply happen by coincidence, but His timing is perfect to work all things together for good.

This can be our story, for God will not only carry us through our tough times, but He will give us favor like the

Shunammite woman. God can do awe-inspiring things, far more than we could ask, hope, or imagine.

And He Cried Out

But Jehoshaphat cried out, and the Lord helped him.

2 Chronicles 18:31 (KJV)

In 2 Chronicles 18, we read about Jehoshaphat. He had the heart for God when he started his reign in Judah. He fortified his army and introduced religious and political reforms. He gained not only honor but prosperity. Jehoshaphat abolished pagan and idol worship in Judah, while his neighbor, the king of Israel, Ahab, introduced the worship of Baal and pagan gods. Then Jehoshaphat made an alliance with King Ahab, who had opposite kingdom principles. Through this friendship, Ahab persuaded him that they would join their forces and go to war against another nation. And Jehoshaphat agreed when he said, "I am as you are, and my people as your people; we will be with you in the war" (2 Chronicles 18:3, WEB).

And the two kings strategized. Jehoshaphat suggested seeking the Lord's will on the matter, so Ahab called on his 400 prophets of Baal, and the answer was a unanimous yes, giving them the assurance of victory. Somehow, Jehoshaphat was not convinced and asked for the prophet of God. But contrary to all the other prophets, he said, "It was doomed," and that death and disaster were waiting on the battlefield. How could 400 prophets be wrong and only one right?

Jehoshaphat disregarded the prophet's warning and went along with the majority to honor his commitment to Ahab.

The battle became fierce, and Jehoshaphat was surrounded by enemy soldiers. Jehoshaphat cried out to God for help, and the Lord helped him and diverted those who pursued him, so they turned back. The battle was a catastrophe. Ahab was killed, and Jehoshaphat escaped—by God's grace and intervention.

Jehoshaphat was bold and faithful to God, but when he aligned with someone with deceitful motives, he followed the world's ways so that he failed to see the negative consequences of his action.

Let us be careful when we partner with someone in rebellion or become a partner in that person's sin and fight a battle we are not supposed to fight. It can be tragic and hasten the death of our friend.

No matter how much we say we love God, if we do not break away from the deception of ungodly friends, we, too, can ignore God's Word, and they can set us up to hand us over to the enemy for death and destruction.

But the Lord is always faithful to hear our cries that when we call on Him, He comes with His saving grace.

But Our Eyes Are on You

*Jehoshaphat was terrified by this news
and begged the Lord for guidance...*

2 Chronicles 20:3 (NLT)

Have you ever been in a situation where you do not know what to do? You are overwhelmed. The problem you are facing is beyond anything you can resolve. No matter what or how you try, nothing works. Discouragement and fear start to settle in. You are in a dilemma. Who can you turn to?

In 2 Chronicles 20, Jehoshaphat was faced with an alliance of three armies marching against Judah. Jehoshaphat and his army were no match for these superpowers. The enemy advanced and surrounded them. Not knowing where and when the enemy would strike was terrifying. Jehoshaphat humbled himself, stood before his people, and confessed that he did not know what to do. He prayed: "For we are powerless before this vast number that comes to fight against us. We do not know what to do, but we look to You" (2 Chronicles 20:12, HCSB). Silence. Deafening silence as the people of Judah stood before the Lord.

The Lord answered,

> Ye shall not need to fight in this battle: set yourselves, stand ye still, and see the salvation

of the Lord with you, O Judah and Jerusalem:
fear not, nor be dismayed; to morrow go out
against them: for the Lord will be with you.

2 Chronicles 20:17 (KJV)

God knew the plans of the enemy just as He saw
Jehoshaphat's humility and heard his cries. God sees and
knows even the deepest thoughts of man.

If God was fighting this battle, did Jehoshaphat and his
men ever wonder why they still had to go to the frontlines
and face the enemy? They may not have fully understood
this strategy, but they obeyed. So, Jehoshaphat went ahead
with a group of singers and, as they began singing praises
to the Lord, suddenly, there came great confusion that the
multitude of the enemy army turned against each other.

When we experience trying circumstances, we respond
in a particular way that we are wired. Maybe, we run to
friends and others we trust and use prayer as our last resort,
but we can learn from Jehoshaphat.

Let's come and humble ourselves to God. In our weakness,
we find refuge and strength in the One who is greater. As
we keep our gaze on the Lord, He removes every fear and
shows us His perspective of our future so that we can face
our struggles, whether in health, relationship, or finances.
Then, we, too, will see that the enemy we feared has become
weak and powerless like pieces of paper being blown by the

mighty wind of God, scattered, tread on, and crushed.

And we can say, "Through God we will do valiantly, for it is he who will tread down our adversaries" (Psalm 60:12, WEB).

The Valley of Berakah

*They took plunder for three days, it was so much.
On the fourth day, they assembled themselves in
Beracah Valley, for there they blessed Yahweh.
Therefore the name of that place was called
"Beracah Valley" to this day.*

2 Chronicles 20:25–26 (WEB)

We learned in 2 Chronicles 20 how three strong armies banded together with threats of total destruction against Jehoshaphat. He feared knowing that they were not only surrounded but outnumbered, and there was no way his army could win against these powerful armies.

In today's world, we also face troubles in health, relationships, and finances, and the attack is beyond what we can take. We find ourselves in the middle of impossible situations that shake us into deep fear and insecurity. We feel weak and lost and find our faith so challenged that no matter how we try to be strong, some are disappointed, discouraged, and others—hopeless. We fear not only for ourselves but also for our loved ones. Yes, in our world today, we face an enemy who wants to steal, kill, and destroy (John 10:10) and an adversary, the devil, who comes like a roaring lion waiting to devour (1 Peter 5:8).

In the face of this real and terrifying threat was only death and destruction. So, Jehoshaphat came before the Lord knowing and trusting in the power of his God as greater than the most powerful army.

We, too, can be in that dark valley, and all we can do is gather some faint strength to pray and say, "Lord, I don't know what to do. I am afraid. There is no way I can fight this battle on my own, but God, I look to You. You are my refuge, my strength, my present help in this time of trouble. Come and help me."

It seems illogical, but God told Jehoshaphat to let the choir go to the frontline and sing. As Jehoshaphat and the people began to sing praises, the Lord set ambushes that caused chaos and confusion, and the enemy started fighting among themselves. When Jehoshaphat's army came, they found them all lying on the ground. It took three days for the men to gather their plunder.

No matter what is happening around us in the natural world, when we are at the lowest points in our lives, when we come to God in humility with prayer and praise, He is faithful to fight our battles.

So, on the fourth day, they gathered again to give thanks and praise to the Lord for their victory and for all that God had done for them. They named this place the valley of Berakah, the "place of blessings."

And the *valley of blessings* still exists today for you and me. We, too, have a miracle in the valley of Berakah with God. And there, we will discover our amazing victory with God. So, with a grateful heart, let us thank and sing praises to a mighty and powerful God, our one true source of blessings.

Hidden in a Tent

The Lord shall sell Sisera into the hand of a woman.

Judges 4:9 (KJV)

It was a time of war. The story in Judges 4 was about the twenty-year period when Israel was oppressed by the Canaanites with their mighty army and chariots of iron. Deborah was judging Israel, and Barak was leading the army. Against overwhelming odds, together, they marched against the commander, Sisera. The battle was fierce, but when Sisera saw that his army was losing in spite of their chariots of iron, he took off and abandoned his men to save his life.

He sought refuge in Jael's tent, knowing that Jael and her people were at peace with him. Not much is known about Jael except that she was the wife of a Kenite living in a tent, living a nomadic lifestyle. Sisera was confident that no one would look for him in a woman's tent. Then he said to her, "I am thirsty. Please give me a little water to drink." Instead, she opened a jug of milk and covered him. Then he said, "If any man comes and inquires of you, and says, is there any man here? You shall say no" (Judges 4:19–20, paraphrased).

Jael not only welcomed him with utmost hospitality but made him feel safe. But Jael knew what she ought to do and wasted no time. When Sisera fell asleep, she used the only tool she had. She took and hammered a tent peg into his head that killed him. What a treacherous and gruesome act!

Today, you and I may be facing another battle, the battle of sin. Jael's story is an image of how to fight our spiritual battles. As it is written in Ephesians 6:12 (HCSB): "For our battle is not against flesh and blood, but against the rulers, against the authorities, against the world powers of this darkness, against the spiritual forces of evil in the heavens."

What doors have we opened to allow the enemy to be comfortable in our life? What friendship are we cultivating that draws us away from our relationship with God? Like Sisera, who told Jael not to tell anyone of his presence, whose words are we listening to? What secrets are we holding on to?

How long do we have to wait? We, too, can take what we have in our hands. We have a *word*, a *promise*. God already knows ahead of time everything that we will go through, so He encourages us to run to Him.

"So be strong and of good courage, do not fear nor be afraid of them; for the Lord your God, He is the One who goes with you. He will not leave you nor forsake you" (Deuteronomy 31:6, NKJV).

We may be alone and hidden in our corner but take that word of God as the powerful hammer that brings healing, restoration of relationships, provision, and victory over every power of the enemy.

"'Is not My word like a fire?' says the Lord, 'And like a hammer that breaks the rock in pieces?'" (Jeremiah 23:29, NKJV).

Hiding in the Winepress

*Gideon threshed wheat by the winepress,
to hide it from the Midianites.*

Judges 6:11 (KJV)

In Judges 6, we find Gideon, the timid, threshing wheat in the winepress. The winepress is for crushing grapes, and Gideon knew that, but he did that to hide from the Midianites. They were the enemy of Gideon's people, who oppressed, attacked, and plundered them during harvest times.

Gideon felt discouraged, fearful, helpless, and stuck, not knowing what to do with their circumstances. He felt powerless to do anything about it. And God heard the cries of the Israelites, so He sent an angel to Gideon. Strangely, everything that the angel said, Gideon felt the opposite. The angel called Gideon a mighty warrior, but Gideon said he was the weakest and the least in his father's house. He wondered if this angel came to the wrong person because the angel told him that he would save the Israelites from the Midianites. Then the angel said, "Surely I will be with you, and you shall strike the Midianites as one man" (Judges 6:16, WEB). But he had nothing to offer. Gideon focused on how small and insignificant he was. He was a nobody. Gideon could not see himself the way God saw him. But in Judges 6:34, the Spirit of the Lord filled Gideon, strengthening him to lead a handful of men and defeat a great army.

There remain Midianites in our world. They come to oppress and intimidate us into such fear and also lead us to do things we're not supposed to do.

"But I will be with you." God's promise is that He never sends us to fight our battle alone and rely on our own strength. With a mighty and powerful God on our side, the weakest man can do great things, and all God wants is our willingness to go where He sends us.

We can go through distressing times over health, marriage, family, or finances. God sees us when we're on our threshing floor. Let God's wind separate the grain from the chaff. He wants to take us out of that place of obscurity where we see ourselves as He sees us. He already knows our every weakness, so He gives us the strength to first face our fear so we can take our stand, knowing that "your God is he who goes with you, to fight for you against your enemies, to save you" (Deuteronomy 20:4, KJV).

Gideon's Weapons of Warfare

[...] and he put into the hands of all them trumpets
and empty pitchers, with torches within the pitchers.

Judges 7:16 (WEB)

We learned how the Midianites were oppressing the Israelites for seven years, so God called Gideon. In Judges 7, Gideon then sent out word for the men to enlist in the army to fight with him. Then came 32,000 men, but the Lord told Gideon to pick only 300 and send the rest home or many of them will brag of their victory because of their own strength.

The Weapons

1. a trumpet,
2. a burning torch inside a clay jar,
3. the battle cry, "A sword for the Lord and for Gideon."

The Battle Plan and the Attack

Gideon divided the 300 men into three groups of a hundred men. Gideon and the hundred men who were with him quietly moved into the Midianite camp while the rest of the group took their places. The Midianites were all asleep except a few of their watchmen. At midnight, when Gideon blew his trumpet as his signal, all the rest of his men blasted their trumpets at the same time. Then they broke the jars in their left hands and shouted, "A sword for the Lord and for Gideon" (Judges 7:20, KJV). The blasts of the trumpets and the crashing of the pitchers as the flames burned brightly from the torches in the dark night seemed like a huge army surrounding the Midianites. The Midianites woke up in terror and fled. And the Lord set each Midianite man in the army against each other.

For you and me.

Is there also a Midianite coming against us?

When God told Gideon to use a trumpet, a torch, and a clay jar, Gideon did not question nor doubt God's strategy. "God chose the foolish things of the world that he might put to shame those who are wise. God chose the weak things of the world that he might put to shame the things that are strong" (1 Corinthians 1:27, WEB).

We are like clay jars, earthen and broken vessels, holding the fire of God inside of us. Even when we are fearful, desperate, or hopeless, the flaming light of God shines through our brokenness to give us the supernatural power to make us His mighty warrior. We can trumpet God's word as our sword to fight against intimidation and oppression over our health, marriage, family relationships, and finances. With God on our side, there can be no other option but a victory for us. As it is written that "the Lord will cause the enemies who rise up against you to be defeated before you. They will march out against you from one direction but flee from you in seven directions" (Deuteronomy 28:7, HCSB). And this is our confidence because the One who promised is faithful.

The Road to Timnah

*Then Samson went down to Timnah with his father
and his mother, and came to the vineyards of Timnah.*

Judges 14:5 (WEB)

The epic story of Samson, as described in the book of Judges 13–16, was a period in history where everyone did what was right in his own eyes, so God raised Samson to deliver the Israelites from the forty-year oppression of the Philistines. God's destiny for Samson was defined even before he was born to be a Nazarite. A call to an ordinary man for conduct and lifestyle greater than himself.

It all began on the way to Timnah by the border between Judah and Philistia, where people of varying cultural backgrounds lived. As soon as Samson saw a Philistine woman, he decided to marry her. This gives us a sense of the direction of Samson's life. He went down the road of contradiction, willfulness, and compromise.

Then, while Samson passed by the vineyards of Timnah, a young lion came roaring and charged at him. And the *Spirit of God came on him* powerfully, and he slew the lion with his bare hands. Here, he discovered his incredible, God-given strength.

In our day, the road to Timnah is also well traveled. Crowded streets are lined with things that appeal to the heart and the imagination.

There will be *vineyards* that offer the finest things of this world. Samson wandered through those vineyards and did things because they looked good. Things are not always as they seem. But God always provides a way out.

The lion appeared while Samson was in the vineyards. We, too, encounter circumstances that shake our confidence, but with God, we can discover hidden strength in the Lord.

Compromise whispers with words that dull the conscience and faints the inner voice of right and wrong. Do we justify our actions?

Temptation tests willpower. Proverbs 6:27 (WEB) also warns, "Can a man take fire in his bosom, and his clothes not be burned?" Samson looked for love in the wrong places. He couldn't resist it. He's a strong man. What could possibly go wrong?

Can the Spirit of God come upon an unrighteous man? In several instances, the story says the "Spirit of God came upon Samson powerfully." Even in those situations where Samson lost sight of his calling and used his gift for personal gain and revenge, God allowed it to demonstrate His glory. May we never lose sight of our calling! And in our times of weakness, we can ask the *Spirit of God* to come upon us to give us that extraordinary strength to resist temptation, give us wisdom, direction, and the power to stand and defeat our enemy for God's glory.

The Valley of Sorek

And she made him sleep upon her knees; and she called for a man, and she caused him to shave off the seven locks of his head; and she began to afflict him, and his strength went from him.

Judges 16:19 (KJV)

In Judges 16, we go with Samson to the valley of Sorek.

The valley of Sorek was at the border of the enemy camp of the Philistines. Samson dared to cross the boundaries, and there, he met and fell in love with Delilah. Though he was a man of supernatural strength to slay a lion with his bare hands and kill a thousand men, he had no willpower to resist the charm and seduction of Delilah. Five Philistine leaders paid Delilah 5,500 pieces of silver to find the secret of his strength so they could overpower and kill him. After many attempts, she succeeded in winning his trust, and he revealed the secret of his strength. And so, in the valley of Sorek, Samson was betrayed by the woman he loved and captured, imprisoned, and enslaved by his enemies. There, Samson lost his physical sight and his true identity in God. While in solitude, he realized what he could not see in the physical, and he asked God for a second chance. God restored his supernatural strength, and Samson won his final victory.

We, too, can travel to the valley of Sorek. It may be a trap of the enemy to derail us from fulfilling God's call over our life. Sometimes, we make poor choices because what looks good or right may not always be as it seems. The spirit of Delilah is persuasive, charming, and seductive. But the power of the spirit of Delilah lies in the condition of the heart of the one being tempted. Often this spirit works to discover our weaknesses while working with other powerful demonic spirits solely with the intention to steal, kill, and destroy.

Self-indulgence is part of humanity's fallen nature, so we need to be vigilant in guarding our hearts. Let us not deceive ourselves by using this weakness as an excuse to commit a sin and blaming the devil. Instead, let this be our strong warning.

Even so, life in today's world continues to have many challenges. If we cross the boundary lines and find ourselves in the valley of Sorek, God is watching us. God knows where we are, and when we call on Him, He will give us the strength to resist that temptation.

Many of the tests we experience are not unusual to men. God is faithful. He sees our hearts and will not allow us to be tempted beyond what we can handle but shows us a way out (1 Corinthians 10:13).

This Time It Will Be Different

Shall we go up again to fight against the Benjamites,
our fellow Israelites, or not?

Judges 20:28 (NIV)

In Judges 20, we learn that there was trouble in the family. Benjamin, the youngest of the twelve sons of Jacob, aligned in a friendship with the men from Gibeah that brought division in the family. The brothers tried to resolve the crisis peacefully and preserve the family unity, but Benjamin stood his ground against them.

A civil war was inevitable between the Israelites and the tribe of Benjamin—each one fighting for a righteous cause. They asked the Lord who should go first, and God told them to let Judah go first. And, very early the following morning, the Israelites went into battle against the Benjamites, but they were defeated.

And, on the second day, the Israelites wept before the Lord and inquired if they should go and attack the Benjamites again, and the Lord told them: "Go up against him" (Judges 20:23, WEB). And so, the Israelites rushed to advance again as they did the first day. And they were defeated again.

This time, on the third day, the Israelites sat before the Lord until evening, offered their burnt sacrifice, and fasted. Then they inquired if they should attack again. This time, they did not rush off to battle until they received the strategy that they were to set an ambush. This time, they waited for confirmation and assurance of victory. And this time, they heard the Lord say, "Go up against him for tomorrow I will deliver him into your hand" (Judges 20:28, WEB). And though the battle was fierce, this time, the Israelites won.

We, too, can be in a fierce battle for that ministry, business, career, or relationship. We know that we are pursuing a righteous cause. We seek the Lord, and yet, we are encountering many hindrances. We are beginning to doubt if we heard right. Our enemy is winning against us. It is not enough to have a reason and good intentions. We need God's clear guidance concerning a given assignment, even for those deep burdens in our hearts, to right the wrongs.

When God calls, He does not leave us groping, wondering what to do. He equips, qualifies, and even aligns the right connections needed to fulfill the role. It is not the size, number, and strength that will win the battle. He delights in our coming to Him, for when we are in that secret place, there, He reveals unknown mysteries. He shows us to perceive through His lens. As we linger in His presence, He touches our hearts so that we begin to love with His love and compassion.

It is by the Spirit of God that we have reconciliation and victory.

The Best Is Yet to Come

Blessed be the Lord, who has not left you
this day without a close relative;
and may his name be famous in Israel!

Ruth 4:14 (NKJV)

We are familiar with the stories of Abraham, Joseph, Moses, and David, to name a few, and how each one of them had a promise, a dream, and a vision. God had a purpose for each one of them, and through time and through many adversities, God was able to connect their individual lives to the greater purpose in God's kingdom. With obedience and faith, each one of them was an important piece in the bigger landscape of God's plan.

Today, we look at Naomi and her family, who left Judea because of famine. While in Moab, Naomi's husband died, and her sons, who married Moabite women, also died, leaving the two widows with her. Naomi, with no means of financial support, hoped to find mercy back among her own people in Bethlehem. But Ruth clung to her, and together, the two widows struggled to make ends meet. Ruth went to gather scraps by the sidelines of Boaz's field, a wealthy landowner. Boaz and Ruth got married, and soon after, they had a son. And in that small village, lives were rearranged and transformed when Naomi held that little baby boy in her arms. And that once despondent and empty home was now filled with the baby's sounds and the lilting lullabies of Naomi. And Naomi's laughter and joy went beyond the confines of her home; it spread through the village.

Naomi lived her life through many difficulties: famine, death, grief, bitterness, heartache, hardship, loneliness, insecurity, and hopelessness. But God, in His sovereign love and grace, was able to weave through her circumstances and poured His grace that changed the course and destiny, not only for Naomi and Ruth but also for thousands of generations, including you and me. Everything that happened to Naomi in her later years, like Ruth, who gleaned in the fields to take care of her and her grandson, who became the grandfather of King David and the ancestor of Jesus, are all part of something bigger than she could have ever imagined.

So, hold onto God's promises, for though we may have some delays and setbacks, God is faithful to bring people into our lives and weave through each of our circumstances so that restoration that brings greater joy and greater increase is ours.

To the young: keep your hope and visions alive, and to the old: believe in your dreams, for the best is yet to come.

And God Remembered Hannah

[...] and the Lord remembered her.

1 Samuel 1:19 (KJV)

"And God remembered [...]" occurs many times in the Bible: with *Noah* (Genesis 8:1), *Abraham* (Genesis 19:29), *Rachel* (Genesis 30:22), to name just a few, and "God remembered *Hannah*" (1 Samuel 1:19).

What does it mean when we read "And God remembered"? Did He really forget? And what about you and me? Do you wonder if God has forgotten you?

Isaiah 49:15 (WEB) says, "Can a woman forget her nursing child, that she should not have compassion on the son of her womb? Yes, these may forget, yet I will not forget you!"

The story of Hannah is found in 1 Samuel, chapter one. Hannah had so many problems. Ridiculed and taunted by Phinehas, she grieved over her barrenness; and her husband tried to shower her with material things because he never fully understood the depth of her pain. During the yearly feasts, Hannah chose to pray in the temple. She cried and poured her heart to God during those times. She continued

137

to believe that God understood her pain. At that moment, she shifted her focus from her desire to have a child for herself to, rather, a spiritual sacrifice to God. She promised the Lord that she would dedicate her son to serve God all the days of his life. She continued to believe that God is bigger than her circumstance and that what is impossible for man, God is able. During one of Hannah's fervent times of supplication to the Lord, Eli, the priest, came and accused her of being drunk. When she explained her plight, Eli told her, "Go in peace, and may God grant your request." Hannah left with inner peace and received the Lord's promise with faith. She went back to the temple the next morning, and this time she worshiped. She went from hopelessness to faith. Verse 19 says, "And the Lord remembered Hannah" (1 Samuel 1:19, paraphrased). And after a time, she bore a son.

The Hebrew word for "remember" is *zakar*.[3]

Hannah chose to come to God in her most vulnerable time. When God saw the change in her heart from a selfish desire to a selfless heart of putting God first, *God remembered* Hannah. God answered her prayer and healed her barrenness.

So today, let's take one more step and choose to align our hearts' desires and motives to the plans and purposes of God. No matter what problem, opposition, obstacle, or disappointment we may be dealing with, we should cry out

---

[3] James Strong, *New Strong's Exhaustive Concordance of the Bible* (Nashville, TN: Thomas Nelson Publishers, 1990), s.v. "zakar."

and pour our hearts before the Lord. As we come to God, we need to trust and believe that nothing is too hard for Him. As we do, let us watch as He brings healing, provision, and restoration to turn things around and gives us the desires of our hearts. Let us worship Him, and may the God of the impossible "zakar" us.

The Lion and the Bear

The Lord that delivered me out of the paw of the lion,
and out of the paw of the bear,
he will deliver me out of the hand of this Philistine.

1 Samuel 17:37 (KJV)

David was the youngest of eight sons who took care of his father's sheep while his three oldest brothers served in the military. One day, his father sent him to bring gifts from home and to check on what was going on with his brothers. He arrived at the camp as Saul's army was in battle formation facing the Philistines. Goliath taunted and mocked Saul and his army. He challenged Saul to send out a champion of their army for a duel between the two armies, but Saul and his men were terrified and retreated (1 Samuel 17:4–11).

In any competition, if we can strike fear through our words to our opponent, we have already won the battle.

David asked questions and volunteered to take the challenge, but his brothers rebuked him. They were angry, accusing him of being prideful and overconfident with evil in his heart. Saul was reluctant, seeing how young and inexperienced David was. But David convinced him how he killed lions and bears that attempted to steal his sheep.

David stood his ground and fought the lion and the bear and refused to let a predator take any of his sheep. The lion and the bear became his preparations for a bigger battle that he was not even aware of. If he had run away from the lion and the bear, he would not have been able to face Goliath. It is written in Luke 16:10 (KJV) that "He that is faithful in that which is least is faithful also in much…" And because of his faithfulness, God strengthened him.

We remember the story of David and Goliath as an analogy of faith to overcome times of adversity that threaten our existence and forget about the lion and the bear.

We, too, have a lion and a bear. Many times, our daily chores and challenges could be a preparation to overcome bigger challenges. Let's not ever undervalue the everyday experiences we encounter along the way. We may not see how God is going to use our past, and we may not know the bigger things that God has prepared for tomorrow, but where we are right now are our stepping-stones to what's coming ahead. There may even be those who don't have any idea of our struggles but will tell us we're not good enough. We can't allow those negative voices to block our advancement. When we are weary in battle, no one else may be there with us, but God sees our faithfulness in the small things. And He knows the perfect timing to bring us out from where we've been hidden to slay that giant in our new place of greater victory.

The Valley of Elah

Now Saul, and they, and all the men of Israel, were in the valley of Elah, fighting with the Philistines.

1 Samuel 17:19 (KJV)

The places we visit can become a significant part of our journey in overcoming our giants. It was just another day when David went to the valley of Elah. David did not come to be a hero, but this uneventful day in the valley became unforgettable and changed his life forever.

The valley of Elah is surrounded by green hills. It may seem like there was nothing special about this valley, but it runs between the hill of the Philistines and the hill of Judah. It became a strategic place, for whoever won the battle would reign over this region.

In this story, we see David preparing to face Goliath. Goliath stood to threaten their existence. David had to get away from the other voices of intimidation, mistrust, and rebuke, even from those on his side, so he went to the brook. Scattered on this stream bed were many things, but he went to pick up five smooth stones for his slingshot as his weapon with the one big God as his secret weapon. David knew that it was not the size of his weapons but his faith in God that mattered. He went into battle with the full confidence of his victory.

We do not have to strive for that extraordinary day, that once-in-a-lifetime experience. When we are faithful in the small things, God can use the hidden, the weakest, and the least in extraordinary ways to accomplish great things. Whatever we're going through, there is a valley of Elah that separates us from the noise and the voice of intimidation and fear. We can pick up our stones of grace by the stream from the brook in that valley.

This battle in the hidden valley of Elah was one of the greatest in biblical history, but many do not remember this battleground.

Many great battles are often won in hidden places.

Facing Your Giant

Choose a man for yourselves, and let him come down to me. If he is able to fight with me and kill me, then will we be your servants.

1 Samuel 17:8–9 (WEB)

We learned that the Philistine army camped on one side of the mountain while Saul and his army gathered on the other side. So, here we continue with David as he faced Goliath.

Having no other options, Saul agreed to let David fight and clothed David with his own armor: his bronze helmet, along with his sword. But after trying them on, David refused to wear Saul's armor. He said, "I cannot go with these, for I have not tested them" (1 Samuel 17:39, WEB). We cannot walk in someone else's shoes and fight with someone else's armor.

Only a ruddy, young shepherd boy stood to defy Goliath. They both stood in the middle ground in that valley of Elah. It was the "winner takes all" fight.

Saul may have slain thousands with his sword, but David's battles were fought with his slingshot and stone. In the eyes of his enemy and with the rest of the soldiers, his strategy defied modern warfare technology. Though David knew this fight was in the flesh, his secret weapon was that he trusted in the Lord. God is bigger than this giant he was facing.

The greatest battle of a young shepherd boy's life was fought out of being alone with God and his sheep, where he learned to kill a lion and a bear with mere stones and a slingshot. Fighting those predators was a daily experience as a shepherd, but David's faith grew as he gained more experience. David had no idea that God would use those times as a training ground for him to slay a fierce giant.

We, too, can face a Goliath that can change our lives forever. We don't know that the very struggles we faced were also our training grounds for the bigger things in our lives. We may have gone through times when we felt abandoned, and all we could do was seek God. It's in those hidden times that we grew, not only in faith but in strength for the new season ahead. We can't allow criticism to stop us. We may not know how to wear armor, but the Lord is our shield. We may not have the sword of Saul, but we have the word of the Lord. We may not have other weapons of warfare, but God will let us use what we have in our hands. God's call for us is one that no one else can do better. When we submit to the lordship of God, the enemy has no power, for the battle becomes the Lord's. With God, with one stone, we can slay a giant right before the eyes of the greatest armies in the world, and they will surely know that God is with us.

The Stronghold in the Cave of Adullam

David left Gath and escaped to the cave of Adullam.

1 Samuel 22:1 (NIV)

There was so much going on in David's life. One season, he was a shepherd boy, then he was anointed as king of Israel, fought a giant, got married, and became a fugitive fearing for his life because of Saul. If God chose him to be the king of Israel, why did he have to run for his life?

With nowhere else to go, David sought refuge in the cave of Adullam. Soon his brothers and his other relatives joined him there. And others also came, men who were in distress, in debt, and discontented (1 Samuel 22:2). People gather around each other who are going through miseries and tend to reinforce the painful situations they're going through. Would he have chosen these men if he had a choice?

David and his men needed a place to hide from all the trauma and pain that life had brought them. Through their imperfections, David and his 400 men banded and stayed together in that cave of Adullam as their refuge and stronghold to become an army. There, they became mighty men of valor, men trained for war, who could handle the shield and spear, whose faces were like the faces of lions, and were as swift as gazelles on the mountains (1 Chronicles 12:8).

But God's word to David was, "Don't stay in the stronghold but go to Judah" (1 Samuel 22:5). The cave of Adullam became their hiding place, giving them a sense of protection. But this place of security can be a place of limitation to hide from the painful realities of life, which only heightens fear and despair.

David and his men were not meant to settle in the cave of Adullam. He was destined to reign as a king with a powerful and loyal army. They had an assignment. When God gives us an assignment, He also gives us a strategy to accomplish that assignment—David and his men were told to go to Judah.

We, too, can be facing a difficult situation. In our darkest time, we can escape to our cave of Adullam for a season. But we are not meant to settle in the stronghold of fear, depression, and despair. God, who is our refuge and strength, will also lead us to Judah, the heart of *praise* (Genesis 29:35).

Praise is a lifestyle. It's a life of surrender, an expression of faith to God. It's a battlefield. It changes us to direct our focus on God to right the wrongs. It tears down walls of fear, frustration, failure, and despair. It takes down the enemy of our soul and raises up and builds our confidence in God to fight the battle for us.

And God is also saying to us, "Get out of that stronghold and go to Judah."

When You're in Ziklag

And David recovered all that the Amalekites
had carried away...

1 Samuel 30:18 (KJV)

After David and his men came out of the cave of Adullam, they were given refuge by a Philistine army leader to stay in the Philistine territory of Ziklag.

It was one of those days when David and his men were called into battle, but after a three-day journey back, the men found their homes burned down and totally destroyed while their wives and children were taken captive. Exhausted and overcome with grief, David and his men wept loudly until they had no power and could not cry anymore (1 Samuel 30:4).

Years of solidarity and closeness were broken by that moment of grief when it turned to anger and bitterness. They blamed David and talked of stoning him. David found himself in a very difficult situation. Not only did he have to face his grief and loss alone, but he also feared for his own life (1 Samuel 30:5–6).

Did you ever experience a time when everything seemed broken and impossible to fix, beyond what you could think or do? You suddenly find yourself alone with no one to turn to, or when those you turn to for comfort have also turned their backs on you? If you are in that Ziklag experience, see what David did.

"David encouraged himself in the Lord his God" (1 Samuel 30:6, KJV). Through his grief, pain, and loss, David was also faced with death threats from his trusted men. But David looked to God. As a seasoned soldier, he did not rely on his ability and experience but totally relied on God to tell him what to do (1 Samuel 30:8). The Lord replied, "Pursue: for thou shalt surely overtake them, and without fail recover all" (1 Samuel 30:8, KJV). David trusted and obeyed God without a doubt. And surely, as God promised, they recovered all and more!

There is only so much we can do. When we focus on our circumstance, we invite fear and lose hope. When we look to others for help, we may encounter betrayal and disappointment. But like David, we, too, can encourage ourselves. Remember those times when God stood by us, times when we once said, "If it had not been the Lord, I don't know what I would have done." In Psalm 56:3 (KJV), David said, "When I am afraid, I will trust in you."

Regardless of what we're feeling, when we choose to come to the Lord with our every burden and allow Him to guide us and direct our steps, when we follow where He leads, He restores. Not only does He give what was lost, but He gives rewards from the enemy.

Listen to the Sound in the Mulberry Trees

And it shall be, when you hear the sound of marching in the tops of the mulberry trees, then you shall advance quickly. For then the Lord will go out before you to strike the camp of the Philistines.

2 Samuel 5:24 (NKJV)

We remember the famous story of David and Goliath. David was a young shepherd boy when he faced the Philistine giant. Years later, when the Philistines heard that David was anointed as king, they went and searched for him in full force, but David heard about it and went down to the stronghold (2 Samuel 5:17–19). The Philistine army camped in the valley of Rephaim. David sought God for direction, and the Lord told him to attack, and David defeated the Philistines. But the Philistines came back and positioned themselves in the valley of Rephaim again. David could have said, "I will fight the Philistines the same way I defeated them before." But, knowing that his victory was of the Lord, he asked God what he should do. God could have also told him, "You know what to do, do it the same way you did the last time you faced them." This time, the Lord told him to circle around behind them and come up in front of the mulberry trees and to wait until he heard the sound of marching in the tops of the mulberry trees (2 Samuel 5:23–24).

Imagine David telling his men, "We need to wait until we hear a marching sound from the mulberry trees. When that happens, get ready for my signal to advance quickly because the Lord will go out before us to strike the enemy." The men must have said among themselves, "Are we hearing him right? 'Marching sounds' from the mulberry trees? What kind of military strategy is that?" But David trusted God, and victory was theirs again.

This story is not about military strategy in battle but an illustration of how David sought the heart and will of God and how he trusted the Lord to guide and direct him in everything that he did.

And today, we, too, can face giants we've battled before that are coming against us in our health, marriage, family, or finances. We make decisions out of emotional impulse, assuming that what we did in the past will work again. The only way we can be assured of overcoming that giant is to come to God for wisdom, direction, and timing. And it does not matter how ridiculous the strategy may look—we can learn from David to do as told. It makes the difference between life or death, success or failure.

David's victories were not won because of his experience or the power of his army but by the Lord. And to this day, God answers our cry for help. Listen to the rushing of the winds in the mulberry trees. He will not only answer our cries, but He comes to fight the battle for us.

As it is written, "Trust in the Lord with all thine heart; and lean not unto thine own understanding. In all thy ways acknowledge him, and he shall direct thy paths" (Proverbs 3:5–6, KJV).

If this story shows us anything, it is not to take any step without God. Do we have the heart to seek God in everything?

He Stayed Home

It happened in the spring of the year, at the time when
kings go out to battle, that David sent Joab [...]
But David remained at Jerusalem.

2 Samuel 11:1 (NKJV)

In biblical times, kings would go into battle in the spring, so David and his men stayed home for a winter break.

It was early in the spring, but David decided to extend his vacation while David's men went to war. We always have the choice to do the things we are called to do or go for something we want. And, oftentimes, we forget that there will be consequences for the choices we make.

One evening, as David got out of bed, he strolled around the roof of the palace and saw a beautiful woman. Temptation comes when we least expect it or when we are at the wrong place at the wrong time. Discernment helps us to distinguish right and wrong, good and evil.

David did not sin by simply seeing the bathing woman. He could have taken his eyes off her and turned around, but he chose to look and followed through by having a sinful relationship with her knowing that both of them were already married. And one sin led to murder when he arranged to have her husband killed in battle (2 Samuel 11:15).

The strength of temptation lies in the condition of the heart and the state of mind of the one being tempted. This temptation was not too strong for David. We know he was a seasoned and powerful warrior. He had the heart of worship for the Lord. This did not just happen. It was something that had been going on in his life, an outcome of a series of incidents. He disregarded God's plan for marriage when he added many other wives. He sowed the seed and cultivated a heart and mind indulging his flesh because he was not satisfied with what God had already given him. What he thought was done in secret and hidden in darkness was all exposed for the world to see, and his sons and daughters suffered the consequences of death, shame, and disgrace (2 Samuel 13).

We, too, will face temptations, and Galatians 5:16 (WEB) teaches us to "walk by the Spirit, and you won't fulfill the lust of the flesh."

The world has shown us many ways of understanding and indulging in the pleasures of life so let us examine our hearts and minds for ungodly things that we have sown and cultivated in the past.

We can ask God for wisdom and to expose hidden weaknesses and strength for pinpoint obedience to what we are called to do.

We can do it because the One who promised is faithful.

Pour Out the Water

*Oh that someone would give me water to drink from
the well of Bethlehem, which is by the gate!*

2 Samuel 23:15 (WEB)

David and his men did great exploits. Second Samuel
23:15–17 tells us a powerful and stirring story of some of
David's mightiest men who risked their lives to grant their
leader's longing for the water from Bethlehem.

When they heard David, the three men crossed the
Philistine lines, took some water out of the well by the gate
in Bethlehem, and brought it back to David. They risked their
lives in extreme danger because of their greater love and
loyalty to their king. David felt grateful for this surprise gift
of love but refused to drink it. He could not enjoy that drink
to satisfy himself. This drink was too costly, so he poured it
out as an offering to the Lord. He said, "The Lord forbid that
I should drink this! This water is as precious as the blood of
these men who risked their lives to bring it to me" (2 Samuel
23:17, NLT).

The act of pouring a drink offering is not a familiar practice
to us. It may seem like a waste of precious and priceless water.
It is like wasting the efforts of those who risked their lives.
The soldiers didn't complain or express how unappreciative
David was for what they did. They understood.

Pouring out an offering to God is an act of worship. A sacrificial offering is an expression of love, obedience, gratitude, faith, and trust that can only be understood in our relationship with God. David understood this drink was more than water. It was as precious as the blood of these men. What greater way could he choose than to make this a sacrificial offering of faith to the Most High God!

David longed for the refreshing water because he was weary from battle. The battles in life can be draining, exhausting, and can be dehydrating. It's in these difficult times that our soul longs for refreshing water. We can get weary and thirsty for a refreshing drink to revive and renew us.

Paul talks about pouring forth a drink offering as a sacrificial offering of faith (Philippians 2:17).

And for you and me today, there is still another well that goes so deep that it never runs dry. It quenches the thirst and the deepest longing of our souls. Jesus said, "If you drink this water, you will never thirst again" (John 4:14, paraphrased).

Come and be refreshed.

Who's on Your Side?

And the Lord sent an angel, which cut off all the
mighty men of valour, and the leaders and captains in
the camp of the king of Assyria. So he returned with
shame of face to his own land.

2 Chronicles 32:21 (KJV)

The king of Assyria threatened not only King Hezekiah and his people but mocked their God by saying, "Don't let your God in whom you trust deceive you, saying, Jerusalem will not be given into the hand of the king of Assyria" (2 Kings 19:10, WEB). He bragged about his victories over every other place he invaded. Then he sent a letter with his army as they were now advancing to attack Hezekiah—psychological weapons to intimidate and discourage Hezekiah. It was a credible threat to bring fear to Hezekiah and his people. But Hezekiah did not consult with any of his council or military leaders; instead, Hezekiah went before the Lord God.

Hezekiah's Strategy (2 Kings 19:14–19)

Verse 14: Hezekiah took the letter and spread it before the Lord. It was his act of surrender and trust in the Lord.

Verse 16: He recognized the greatness of God. Who was this man to mock the living God?

Verse 19: He had the assurance that God cared and would

not abandon him. Hezekiah trusted that the battle was the Lord's and that all the kingdoms of the earth may know that God alone is the Lord God.

We, too, have an enemy that uses intimidation as a weapon of psychological warfare to shake our confidence and trust in God to convince us of demonic logic.

We, too, can face a situation where we are told the worst that could happen, whether it's for our health, marriage, family, or finances. And the threats we are facing are real and can be devastating to shake the little hope within us.

But we can learn from Hezekiah not to trust in our own understanding and strength but that God is great and mighty and that there is no one greater than Him. When we come in faith, He gives us the assurance of victory, as Hezekiah later said, "Be strong and courageous, be not afraid nor dismayed for the king of Assyria, nor for all the multitude that is with him: for there be more with us than with him" (2 Chronicles 32:7, KJV).

If we think we are boxed in and disaster awaits us, there's more to Hezekiah's story. That night, the angel of the Lord went out and killed the 185,000 of the Assyrian army (2 Kings 19:35). Imagine the sight of this powerful, once undefeated army slain even before the battle began. There is no army so powerful and mighty than our God, our defender.

"If God is for us, who can be against us?" (Romans 8:31, WEB).

An Evening with the King

For if you remain silent now, then relief and deliverance will come to the Jews from another place, but you and your father's house will perish. Who knows if you haven't come to the kingdom for such a time as this?

Esther 4:14 (WEB)

The things that happen in our lives may not always be as we hope. Decisions made may result in facing unpleasant situations and difficult people in every way, including marriage and family. And it may not always be our fault.

This was the story of Esther. She was an orphan, an Israelite girl, but her uncle signed her up for a beauty contest to be the queen of the greatest empire in the world. So, Esther, like all the other women, had to go through a time of purification, beautification, intense preparation, and learn the rules of royal etiquette before they were brought for an audience with the king. And through it all, she hid her true identity.

While undergoing training for her new role, she was disconnected from the events beyond her circle in the palace, but she was told of the plot to destroy not only her family but her people. This was a revelation in a critical time, and silence was no longer an option, for who knew that she might have been placed on the throne for such a time as this?

Knowing about the King is not the same as knowing Him.

She knew she could be sentenced to death, yet she defied protocol and dared to come before the presence of her king without being summoned. But as soon as the king saw her standing in the courtyard, he welcomed her and held out the gold scepter to her. So, Esther approached and touched the end of the scepter. Then the king asked her, "What would you like, queen Esther? What is your request? It shall be given you even to the half of the kingdom" (Esther 5:2–3, WEB).

Instead, she arranged a banquet for an evening with the king. This time, she no longer wanted to live in the secrecy of her true identity. She understood the consequences of her actions but trusted in God's grace and mercy, so she humbled and risked her own life. This was bigger than herself, so she pleaded for his intervention to save the lives of many other innocent people. And the heart of the king was moved that he granted her favor.

So, no matter what we've done in the past, whatever we are going through, who knows, we may also be here for such a time as this. And like Esther, when we humble ourselves and depend on the Lord's unmerited favor, we not only stand out in the crowd but receive promotion and favor with God and men.

"For the eyes of the Lord run to and fro throughout the whole earth, to shew himself strong in the behalf of them whose heart is perfect toward him" (2 Chronicles 16:9, KJV).

And like Esther, who found grace and favor before her king, "let us therefore come boldly unto the throne of grace, that we may obtain mercy, and find grace to help in time of need" (Hebrews 4:16, KJV).

The Valley of the Shadow of Death

Even though I walk through the valley of the shadow of death, I will fear no evil, for you are with me. Your rod and your staff, they comfort me.

Psalm 23:4 (WEB)

Will God take you to a place where you don't want to go?

Psalm 23 begins with the "Lord is my Shepherd," a personal relationship between the Shepherd and the sheep. The Shepherd takes care, loves, and looks after the flock and for each and every sheep. He takes them to green pastures and clear water while paying a watchful eye on each sheep so that no one goes astray. A sheep can easily wander and get stuck in a thorny bush, eager to venture beyond the boundaries but can get lost and be snatched by a predator. A sheep is helpless and will not survive without the Shepherd. And so, as God as our Shepherd, we must put ourselves as sheep—in our total dependency on the Shepherd.

But what happens when the Shepherd takes the sheep into a path through the valley of deepest darkness (Psalm 23:4)?

Between the high walls of a hill or a mountain lies a depressed part of the land called the "valley." Even though we walk with the Lord, we can walk through that narrow place and experience dark times of depression, anxiety, and problems that overwhelm us with fear, doubt, and insecurity. Times when we feel alone, lonely, and fearful because our contending for a breakthrough becomes a struggle toward our Shepherd. We have a promise of healing and restoration, but where is *our* promise?

We wrestle with our emotions and our faith to believe not just the promise but the One who promised.

What do we do when the prayers we have been praying for don't seem to be answered, when things that we are believing for seem over and there's nothing we can do? Doctors are saying, "We've done everything we can." Our son or daughter has run away from the family; the marriage has reached the end; we don't know how our life is going to be. When we are in the valley facing those most difficult times and cry, God, where are You? Yet the Good Shepherd is right beside us. It's a lonely place.

It may only be for a season or for a night, but when we wrestle with our emotions and our faith, we can easily lose hope. We are only passing through the valley. So, don't give up, daybreak is coming like Jacob, who was alone when he wrestled with God through the night, but at daybreak, he received a blessing, a new name, and a new walk.

We wonder and ask, "Why did God let this happen?" We may not fully understand, but through it all, God has already been to our future, so we can say, "I will fear no evil, for You are with me." The Lord, our Shepherd, will guide us through the dark valleys and take us to the wide open and beautiful sunny field. And so, we thank God that "surely goodness and mercy shall follow me all the days of my life: and I will dwell in the house of the Lord for ever" (Psalm 23:6, KJV).

Your Life Story

Every day of my life was recorded in your book. Every moment was laid out before a single day had passed.

Psalm 139:16 (NLT)

Did you ever say or hear someone say, "If I knew then what I know now, I would have done things differently?" You would rather do something else, but you are afraid of the negative consequences. What if? Is there a way to know?

David said, "Lord, You have searched me and known me. You know when I sit down and when I stand up; You understand my thoughts from far away" (Psalm 139:1–2, HCSB).

David's words help us see ourselves from God's perspective. Each of our lives is a storybook. God wrote the pages of our book, so He knows every line, the steps, the leaps, and the tumbles that happen in our lives.

What is your life telling? As the Creator, God knew everything there is to know about you and me even before our mothers and fathers knew us. He knows us more than we know ourselves. We may not always understand the things that are going on in our lives, but God does. God knows every street address of where we have lived. That chance meeting with someone was divinely appointed after all. He knows every path we take in our journey.

Do you wonder if there is a way to know what God wrote in your book? He invites us to ask Him of things to come. He said, "Call to me, and I will answer you, and will show you great and difficult things, which you don't know" (Jeremiah 33:3, WEB).

In the Bible, we read of men and women whose stories were also written by God. We come across a page about David, and though he practiced his lines, he sometimes had to ad-lib, miss his cue, and mess up his lines. Yet many times, he sought the Creator and Director for guidance. He allowed God to navigate his life based on what was written about him.

As we flip through the pages of our book, we will see how we made a wrong turn in that corner, only to find out we were meant to be there. You and I are not some random characters, but God imagined and uniquely thought of us. Maybe we are so used to looking at ourselves that we don't see who God created us to be.

But if we stay in God's word, we will discover new joy and meaning in life's mysteries. And gain wisdom and strength to break through barriers that the villains set up to derail God's storyline. But we can declare, "Wherever I go, your hand will guide me; your strength will empower me" (Psalm 139:10, TPT).

The Valley of Dry Bones

I will put my Spirit in you, and you will live.

Ezekiel 37:14 (WEB)

God took Ezekiel to a valley full of dry, human bones, and He asked, "Son of man, can these bones live?" Ezekiel did not quite answer the question but replied, "O Lord God, you know" (Ezekiel 37:3, NKJV).

Our story in Ezekiel 37 may seem like a scene from some horror movie, so imagine Ezekiel looking at all these dead bones that were not given a proper burial. It was a picture not only of death but of shame and disgrace. This was the story of the house of Israel. It was a dark and depressing period when Israel was under Babylonian captivity but beyond the grim landscape of lifeless bodies is a story of hope.

God could have commanded these bones to be revived and restored, but He asked a man to stand in the gap. So, Ezekiel stood before an audience of dead bones and spoke God's promises of life:

- *"I will cause breath to enter you."*
- *"I will put sinews on you."*
- *"I will make flesh grow on you."*
- *"I will cover you with skin."*
- *"You will live."*

- *"I am going to open your graves and cause you to come out of your graves."*
- *"I will put My Spirit in you."*
- *"I will place you in your own land."*
- *"Then you will know that I am the Lord"* (Ezekiel 37:5–14, paraphrased).

Do words really have power? As we see in this story, words of life were spoken over the dead bones, and they lived. Death has no power over God's love for His people. God wanted to revive His people not only physically but spiritually. He wanted to give them a new heart that beat to a new rhythm. No longer that hard, stubborn, and rebellious heart but one that knows and acknowledges Him as God.

We, too, can be in that valley. And everything that we once had and hoped for, whether in health, relationship, or finances, is lost and gone. Restoration is impossible, and there's just no way of recovering anything other than a miracle.

But we see in the valley of dry bones God's heart and His saving grace that gave new life to the dead and redeemed them from shame and disgrace. We, too, can receive the message of hope of God's saving grace, and though we may be dead in sin (Ephesians 2:1), we can have a new life.

Within the valley of dry bones flows a river of life. And what is impossible with man, God's word has the power to bring revival.

Hear Him say, "You will come alive again."

Unfailing Love

So I bought her for myself for fifteen pieces of silver and a homer and a half of barley.

Hosea 3:2 (WEB)

We meet Hosea, a young preacher who married Gomer. The early days of their marriage were beautiful, and God blessed them with a son. After the birth of their children, Hosea continued to preach while Gomer had other interests, spending more time away from home. Hosea suspected Gomer's unfaithfulness and his heart began to break. His beloved was going off with other men. And Hosea had to face the reality of a broken marriage when Gomer ran off with her lovers, who promised to give her material things (Hosea 2:5) though he found out later that her lovers sold her to slavery.

But God told Hosea to do something that's too hard to understand—to go and redeem his wife. He searched for her and found her in a mess, dirty, and chained for auction at the filthy slave market. This was a contrasting image of the beautiful woman he married and loved. Hosea bought her for fifteen pieces of silver and a homer and a half of barley, brought her back home, and continued loving her as his only beloved wife—with unconditional, forgiving love that changed her to respond and become his faithful wife.

Through Gomer, we see how sin can lead to a life of slavery and bondage, mentally, emotionally, and spiritually. Through Hosea, we see the power of love to overcome the deep wounds of infidelity—the unconditional love to forgive, bringing redemption and restoration. Hosea's unfailing love helped to change Gomer, and she responded with renewed love and became his faithful wife.

The story of Hosea and Gomer is an allegory of God's love for His people. He loves us with an everlasting love. Not even death can separate us from His love (Romans 8:39). His love is unstoppable. We have free will, but His love never changes and never lets go. His love does not count the wrongs. His faithful love is powerful to transform our hearts so that we respond with love to His love.

You and I were not purchased with silver but with the precious blood of Jesus. He paid a price that we cannot repay. And for anyone who has run off after the world and its pleasures, God is still calling, "Come back to your first love."

Jonah and the Whale

But the Lord sent out a great wind into the sea,
and there was a mighty tempest in the sea,
so that the ship was like to be broken.

Jonah 1:4 (KJV)

The story of Jonah and the whale is a familiar and remarkable story of the depth of God's love, grace, and mercy, even to the most undeserving.

It began with a call on Jonah to go to Nineveh, the capital of the Assyrian empire. Historically, Assyria was one of the worst enemies of Israel, but God sent Jonah to deliver a message to the Assyrians in Nineveh to repent from their sinful ways. Why would God send Jonah, a Hebrew, to go to these pagan gentiles? What can we do when we are asked to do something we don't want to do?

Jonah tried to run away from God and boarded a boat heading in the opposite and farthest direction from Nineveh. But the Lord sent a violent storm that threatened to destroy not only the ship but everyone on board, yet Jonah slept until the captain woke him up, saying, "How can you sleep at a time like this?" We have many modern-day "Jonahs" who are asleep to the problems around them and refuse to step out of their comfort zone.

Jonah realized this storm was God's chastisement for his disobedience, and so he told them to throw him overboard. Jonah would rather die and drown. But immediately, the raging waves calmed, and a whale swallowed him, and he stayed in that whale's belly for three days. Jonah did everything to go against God's call and assignment, but there was nowhere to run and hide that God could not see and no prayers spoken that God could not hear. In that cold and dark place, Jonah cried out to God as he prayed a prayer of repentance. And instantly, he found himself out of the whale's belly and on the beach.

God is a God of many chances, for His grace and mercy are far greater even to the worst and least likable people of Nineveh. When Jonah went and preached the gospel, the King and all the people fasted, prayed, and turned from their evil ways. But Jonah was angry. He would have much rather seen them judged and destroyed. He knew God, but his heart was far from God.

God does not want us simply to know about Him. He wants us to know Him.

Oftentimes when we encounter trouble, we are quick to say that we are under some demonic attack, but some of the storms we encounter may be God-sent to interrupt us from going against God's plans. How long are we going to run away from our assignment with the hope that it will go away? Are we like Jonah, avoiding doing them because we can't forgive or because we have certain prejudices? We carry that load that weighs heavier each day until we realize that with one step, it's not that difficult after all. God never gave up on Jonah and the people in Nineveh. In our weakness and defiance, He is patient, kind, and slow to anger to demonstrate His love and grace. And He, too, will never give up on you and me.

They Followed the Star

For we saw his star in the east,
and have come to worship him.

Matthew 2:2 (WEB)

From far away in the East, astrologers saw this bright star. They watched this star as a sign of something that was to happen that would change the world forever. As Isaiah foretold that a virgin would give birth to a son who would deliver Israel (Isaiah 9:6).

It was on this night when the astrologers, also called magi, saw this star in the heavens; they ventured into the unknown and followed the star to the newborn king. When they came into the house and saw a young child with His mother, Mary, they fell on their knees and worshiped Him. Then they opened and presented their gifts of gold, frankincense, and myrrh (Matthew 2:11).

The magi were learned seekers of truth who sought after the One greater than themselves. The first gentiles who risked leaving everything they had to come to Jesus. Today many know about Jesus. But knowing about Jesus is not the same as how we know Him. Life's journey is not always easy when we are faced with delays, opposition, rejection, and hindrances, but think again about what the magi did. Don't settle for the familiar and miss out on the adventure and the joy of discovering something bigger. Press in and go deeper in our relationship with God.

On that dark night, they followed the bright light of that far, far away star. Although darkness surrounds us from some pain and the offenses of what we did or what others did to us, like the magi, let's also focus on the *light*. The Word of God is always there to be a light, encourage, strengthen, guide, and lead us to our destiny.

God can communicate in whatever language we understand. The magi understood the signs in the heavens. And God used a star to lead them to a deeper revelation and understanding and found Jesus.

You and I have a language of understanding that is unique and personal, and God will speak to us individually to draw us closer to Him so that we may find new joy and meaning with a sense of wonder in the miracle of love that God had already given to you and me thousands of years ago even before the magi came.

Let us come, adore, and worship Him with our precious gifts.

What Is God's Will for Me?

Thy will be done in earth, as it is in heaven.

Matthew 6:10 (KJV)

Have you ever experienced times when you were praying and yet God seemed distant or silent that you wondered what the greater purpose in your life was?

The more we spend time and engage in a two-way conversation with someone, the better we get to know and relate to that person. We talk to God when we pray, but do we hear God talking to us?

The disciples watched Jesus pray. There was something different when Jesus prayed, so they asked Him to teach them how to pray. And Jesus taught them the Lord's Prayer (Matthew 6:9–13).

Verse 10 of the Lord's Prayer says, "Your will be done..." When we say, "Your will be done," are we saying, "I will set aside my heart's desire and follow Your word for me," or do we tell God specifics of what and how we want things to happen?

As we read Scripture and let His words marinate in our hearts, we begin to hear God speaking. We can start with one verse and apply it to our lives today. God's Word is honest and powerful to bring healing, prosperity, and success in what we do (Deuteronomy 8:18). He gives us strength (Exodus 15:2). His Word guides and directs us like a light to our path (Psalm 119:105). He has a way of exposing our weakness with sharpness and accuracy, and we wonder how specific this word is. It's at that moment we know God is talking to us.

We have the freedom to plan and do whatever we want at any given time, and the consequences can be beneficial or hard lessons to take. Whether knowingly or unknowingly, we may do things against God's will, yet He honors the choices we make. But when we have a personal and close walk with God and earnestly desire to do His will, we can pray for wisdom and guidance. When we ask God for specifics like where He wants us to live, what job to take, and who to marry, He answers and directs our steps and keeps us from making wrong choices.

Do you know if God has a plan for your life? Yes, God had a dream for you and me when He wrote a storybook about each one of us. God is waiting and eager to share with us things that He wants our hearts to dream with Him. So, if we want to know God's will, Scripture tells us to simply ask Him. He will answer and show us great and impossible things to understand (Jeremiah 33:3). So, we now have the assurance that when we come to Him boldly, knowing that what we're asking for is according to His will, He not only listens but hears and grants us our request (1 John 5:14).

What Do You Want Me to Do for You?

"Lord," they answered, "we want to see."

Matthew 20:33 (NLT)

In Matthew 20:29–34, Jesus and His disciples were leaving Jericho. There were two blind men who were sitting by the sidewalk. They could sense something was going on, and when they heard about Jesus, they called Him, "Son of David, have mercy on us." The crowd tried to quiet them, but they shouted even louder. And Jesus had compassion and stopped in front of them and asked, "What do you want me to do for you?" (Matthew 20:32, WEB).

The blind men called Jesus "Son of David" (2 Samuel 7:12–16). These blind men saw the Messiah in Jesus. They were beggars living in darkness, but this was their only chance to be delivered from their impossible situation. They had the spiritual insight to ask for mercy that Messiah alone could do for them. They refused to be intimidated by the crowd who tried to stop them. Giving up was not an option.

It was obvious the men were blind, but Jesus asked what they wanted from Him. He already knew what they needed, but Jesus wanted them to verbalize their request and their faith in Him as their healer.

What challenges are you facing? We may have challenges in the physical, emotional, relational or mental. We may also have inner questions, and we don't even know what we really want for ourselves. Even those close to us are going to stop or block us from pursuing our desires. We don't have to be defined by our past or present circumstances. God already knows our every need before we even ask Him, but He wants us to come and tell Him our requests (Philippians 4:6). We come to God as our healer, our savior, our deliverer, our strength, our hope, and the giver of new life. It is an act of faith in the One who is greater than us.

The two blind men believed, and because of their faith, Jesus stopped what He was doing to touch them, and they received their miracle.

Let faith arise, and be healed.

One Dark Night
in Gethsemane

He came to the disciples and found them sleeping,
and said to Peter, "What, couldn't you watch
with me for one hour?"

Matthew 26:40 (WEB)

Matthew 26:36–40. It was Thursday night, and Jesus ate His last meal with His beloved disciples. He alluded to many things concerning His departure, including betrayals among them. Later, He went with three of them to the olive grove called Gethsemane. Olives were crushed to facilitate the release of the precious oil. Gethsemane was that place of pressing and crushing.

Jesus handpicked each one of the twelve disciples, but that night, two of them would betray Him. Judas had a position of trust, requiring honesty and integrity with money, and Peter, who professed loyalty and willingness to die for Him, would deny Him three times.

Betrayal is painful and devastating when someone we love violates our trust. Jesus knows. He said, "Even my close friend, someone I trusted, one who shared my bread, has turned against me" (Psalm 41:9, NIV).

We, too, can go through the anguish and distress from the betrayal that cuts a deep wound into our souls. What did Jesus do?

Jesus went to Gethsemane. He knew that His flesh was about to be crushed to release the oil of forgiveness and salvation not only for those who betrayed Him but for all humanity. He said, "My soul is crushed with grief to the point of death" (Matthew 26:38, NLT). He did not hide or ignore His feelings. When we come to Gethsemane as our place of humility, we also crush our flesh, our act of surrender to God.

Jesus prayed. In prayer, we talk to God about our innermost thoughts and feelings. We can reach that point and say, "God, I can't do it on my own," but God always gives us the strength to overcome and forgive.

Jesus forgave. Forgiveness is not a feeling but a choice. Forgiveness is giving our burden to God. When we ask forgiveness for our wrongdoings, we want God's total acceptance, grace, and blessings, but when someone betrays us, we want revenge. We struggle to forgive and bless that betrayer, but the Bible says, "Do not repay evil with evil or insult with insult. On the contrary, repay evil with blessing, because to this you were called so that you may inherit a blessing" (1 Peter 3:9, NIV).

Some say, "I've moved on." The deep wounds of betrayal will not heal by themselves without forgiveness. Unforgiveness brings bitterness with far-reaching poisonous roots. Over time, the poison affects not only one's physical health but relationships with man and God. But through our brokenness, with God, we can truly forgive and be set free.

When the Rooster Crows

Watch and pray, that ye enter not into temptation:
the spirit indeed is willing, but the flesh is weak.

Matthew 26:41 (KJV)

Simon Peter was strong-willed, impulsive, outspoken, and fully convinced of his loyalty and devotion to Jesus. When Jesus told him that that night before the rooster crows, he would deny Him three times, Peter immediately responded, "Even if I must die with you, I will not deny you" (Matthew 26:34–35, WEB).

Jesus knew that the time for His arrest was about to happen, so He took Peter, James, and John to the Garden of Gethsemane to pray. Several times in the night, Jesus came to them, but they were sleeping. Then the soldiers came and arrested Jesus, but Peter followed from a distance. When the crowd lit a fire by the courtyard, Peter sat among them, and a few recognized Peter and pointed him out as a follower of Jesus, but Peter denied knowing Him.

Peter's Denials (Matthew 26:69–74, WEB)

He denied being a Galilean. Peter said, "I don't know what you are talking about."

He denied being a follower of Jesus. Peter said, "I don't know the man."

He denied knowing Jesus. Peter began to curse and swear, "I don't know the man!"

It was only a few hours ago when he professed that he was willing to die for Jesus. Peter left his successful fishing business to follow Jesus. He spent three years of learning and moving in signs, wonders, and miracles that we could only hope to see. So, what made Peter deny Jesus?

Peter was asleep. He slept when he needed to be watchful and praying. We, too, are warned to be alert because our adversary, the devil, prowls around like a roaring lion, looking for anyone to devour (1 Peter 5:8).

Peter was fearful. Fear can lead us to do things contrary to our deepest convictions.

Peter was proud to boast of his willingness to die for Jesus. The disciple whom Jesus chose, loved, and mentored now disowned and betrayed Him. Through the chaos and the crowd, Jesus turned and looked at Peter, and the look in His eyes expressed more than any word He could have spoken. The wounds of betrayal from someone we love and care for are far more painful than the wounds enemies can inflict. Then the cock crowed, and Simon Peter remembered Jesus's words, and he "wept bitterly" (Luke 22:62, WEB).

But Jesus knew his heart.

God sees our hearts too. We also have shortcomings and fail like Simon Peter, but God's mercy and grace abound to give us the hope that God's unconditional love is stronger to forgive and restore us.

The Hill at Golgotha

And when they were come unto a place
called Golgotha, that is to say, a place of a skull...

Matthew 27:33 (KJV)

In Matthew 27, we come to a hill called "the place of the skull." It's where Jesus was crucified. This place of suffering and burial was also called the "hill of Golgotha."

Jesus wore the crown of thorns for the suffering and deep pain in our minds. Our mind is powerful enough to influence our emotions. Our emotions can direct our actions and, ultimately, the way we live our life and redirect the course of our future. As written in Proverbs 23:7 (KJV), "For as he thinks in his heart, so is he." One of the most important things in our lives is our thoughts. Our thoughts have the power to do us good or harm. The things in our lives that lead us to sin do not just happen. It always starts with something small, a word as a seed, an action that grows as we cultivate to indulge the flesh. The flesh cannot please God, and so the mind becomes a battlefield of the flesh and the spirit (Romans 8:7).

Our minds can be *blinded* when a person can be the most knowledgeable in many things, but there's a veil to the mind from spiritual truth. Scripture says that we are to ignore and not entertain evil and wrong thoughts, visions, distorted events, or scenarios that never even happened. We cannot allow those thoughts to be played in our minds and to find ourselves living in a world of make-believe, detached from reality, and filled with lies, negativity, and darkness (2 Corinthians 10:5).

There is also the *doubtful mind*; the book of James talks about a double-minded one who is unstable in all his or her ways. We can't have one foot in the world and the other foot with God. We can ask God to change our attitudes and behavior by allowing God to change the way we think. Only then are we able to understand God's good and perfect will over our lives.

We long for laughter and joy but feel depressed and tormented when our minds become a battlefield of conflicting thoughts, dark, hopeless, and unhappy from a depraved and depressed mind. But Jesus, with His crown of thorns, was on that "hill of the skull" so that we can now wear the crown of gold for a *renewed mind.*

It was on the "hill of skulls" that the battle of the mind was fought, that the head of the serpent was crushed. And to this day, Golgotha is a reminder of Jesus's sacrifice that we have been forgiven, redeemed from death, and reconciled with God so that we no longer dwell on the hill of suffering and pain but live the victoriously abundant life. We have a transformed mind, an enlightened mind with wisdom through the revelation of God, the mind of Christ (1 Corinthians 2:16).

Calming the Storm

The disciples woke him up, shouting,
"Teacher, don't you care that we're going to drown?"

Mark 4:38 (NLT)

The story in Mark 4:35–41 began when Jesus and His disciples were on the shore by the Sea of Galilee.

The sun was setting, the Sea of Galilee was calm, and the surface of the water glistened as light waves swayed the boat. Jesus told His disciples, "Let us cross over to the other side." There were also other boats, both big and small, with them. After a long day of preaching and teaching, Jesus fell asleep in the back of the boat. The shoreline was now covered in darkness by the time they reached the middle of the lake. Then out of nowhere, a sudden unexpected storm appeared. The disciples were experienced fishermen and knew these waters. They rowed hard to steady the boat as fierce winds battered and crashing waves rocked the boat violently up and down with every wave that struck it. They scrambled to ride the waves as they held onto the sides of the boat while they tried to scoop out the water as fast as they could. They knew they were in danger of losing their lives. But Jesus seemed unaware of the chaos and remained asleep. How could he still be sleeping? They woke Him up and asked, "Do you not care? We are drowning." Jesus woke up and said, "Peace be still" (Mark 4:39, WEB), and it was *still*!

In the sea of life, there will be times we sail under the beautiful sunny blue skies on calm and peaceful waters when suddenly darkness overshadows, and we are in the middle of a raging storm. No one of us wants to go through a storm, yet no one of us is exempt from the storms of life. A storm may only be for a season, but a hurricane can be devastating with the sudden death of a loved one or with crippling sickness or physical pain, broken marriage, strained family relationships, or financial crisis. We stretch our faith to steady the boat and stay on course and stay afloat, but the waves of fear can be stronger and threaten to drown us. And we cry out, "Lord, help us."

Jesus asked the disciples, "Why are you so afraid? How is it that you have no faith?" (Mark 4:40, WEB). We don't have to allow the storm and the chaos to govern us. We can call on the One who can calm the storm. With three words, the raging storm was completely tamed. Deliverance came not only to the disciples but to all the other boats that would have perished in that storm.

Far beyond the horizon are endless possibilities for a new discovery, and when God is telling us to cross over to the other side, will we have faith?

Who Touched Me?

Daughter, your faith has made you well.
Go in peace, and be cured of your disease.

Mark 5:34 (WEB)

Hope is an expectation of change. People often say, "I hope so," but that hope conveys a sense of doubt. When the Bible talks about hope, it is often linked with faith in God, which brings a sense of assurance, confidence, and security that what we believe in the spirit, contrary to our circumstance, will happen in the natural world (Hebrews 11:1).

Hope covers many areas in our lives. Mark 5:24–34 (WEB) gives us an illustration to keep on believing for our healing, like the woman who suffered continual bleeding for twelve years. Aside from the financial burden of her treatments and her physical pain, the emotional and mental anguish was more than she could carry. She has had to endure twelve long years of pain and suffering: constantly fearing for her future as her condition progressively worsened and not having enough money for doctor bills. She was considered ceremonially unclean, which means she was restricted from any religious, family, or social gathering. She became an outcast. She was desperate.

Then she heard about Jesus. As usual, a huge crowd followed Jesus, but the woman said to herself, "If I just touch his clothes, I will be made well" (Mark 5:28, WEB). She deeply believed Jesus could heal her, but she could not ask Jesus in front of the crowd, so she crawled to secretly touch the hem of His garment. As soon as she touched him, she felt instant healing. And Jesus also felt that power had gone out of Him, so He asked, "Who touched my clothes?" How could He even ask with people pressing around Him? She had no choice but to step out with fear and, trembling, admit publicly what she did. Jesus already knew what happened, but though He did not mean to embarrass her, He wanted her and others to know that her faith healed her.

God always brings to light things that show the greatness of His work, even those done in secret.

And today, we may be going through painful infirmities and diseases that may not be physically visible but can cloud our thinking to even turn against God and stop believing. But in her pain, the bleeding woman chose to come to Jesus.

Come to Jesus!

Despite her pain and weakness, she gathered what little strength and courage she had to get out of her place of confinement. Ignoring the crowd, she broke through society's rules and restrictions to approach Jesus, believing in the promise of healing. If the woman followed the boundaries placed on her condition and allowed the failures of the past attempts to be healed to determine her future, she would never have received her healing and blessings.

What is holding you back? Break away from man's expectations and the old ways of doing things. Let's not allow our failures in the past to stop us from pursuing God's promises over our life. Her faith used the hem of His clothes to be her contact point, something no one had ever done before. Are we willing to do something we have not done before to pursue our goal? God is faithful to do the impossible we believe for.

Sent into a Storm

Take Courage, It is I.

Mark 6:50 (NIV)

In Mark 6:45–52, we read that after a long day of ministering, Jesus told the disciples to get on the boat and go ahead of Him to the other side of the lake to Bethsaida while He went up to the mountainside to pray.

Then a sudden storm came. From His vantage point, Jesus saw the disciples struggling as they rowed, trying to steady the boat. They were stuck in the middle of the lake, fighting the contrary winds creating a huge wave, and the boat was riding up and down. But Jesus came across the waves to be with them. He said, "Don't be afraid. Take courage! I am here" (Mark 6:50, NIV). As Jesus got into the boat, the wind stopped, and they sailed on to the other side.

Jesus knew there would be a storm. The disciples were experienced fishermen and knew these waters. God knows we will have storms in our lives. Even the most experienced among us will go through a storm. The raging waters can threaten to sink our faith, but we need to press on.

Things are going well, and suddenly, we are hit with an unexpected loss, pain, and disappointment that we get overwhelmed, anxious, and weary. We can trust God is watching us. Could it be that God is using this unexpected circumstance to strengthen our faith that He is a promise keeper? The disciples panicked and forgot that Jesus told them they would get to the other side.

We may be walking in unexpected circumstances where we feel stuck in the middle of nowhere, uncertain, and just don't know what to do, and we begin to doubt our future. We do not walk alone. God knows where we are. No matter how hard we try, we can't do everything right, but He sees our struggles and knows our every weakness. He will get us through.

Whatever we're facing today, God is with us. It doesn't matter how dark the night—when we have a promise from God, He always keeps His promise. He will see us through. Nothing can stop His plan for each one of us.

Lord, Help My Unbelief

*If you can believe, all things are possible
to him who believes.*

Mark 9:23 (WEB)

We read in Mark 9:14–24 about a father who brought his son, who was controlled by a demonic spirit, to the disciples, but they could not cast it out. When Jesus came, and the disciples told Him that they failed, He said, "O faithless generation, [...] bring him unto me" (Mark 9:19, KJV). As soon as the demonic spirit saw Jesus, he threw the boy in a violent convulsion as he fell to the ground, writhing and foaming in his mouth. It was heartbreaking for the father to see the condition of his son. Having no other possible medical alternative, he was desperate and could only hope for a miracle.

He came to Jesus: "If you can do anything, have compassion on us, and help us."

Jesus said, "If you can believe, all things are possible to him who believes."

And the father immediately cried out with tears, "I believe. Help my unbelief!" (Mark 9:22–24, WEB).

Is there a contradiction? Did the father say, I believe but did not really believe? He has faith mixed with some doubt. The father believed that Jesus has the power to heal, but he also needed the faith that his son would be healed. Like that father, we, too, have struggles with doubt. Sometimes, we ask for small things and have great faith because we know it is easy for God. But when it comes to asking for the impossible, we feel the opposite: we have little faith and keep our fingers crossed for God to hear. We have faith and unbelief mixed together when situations that we've been praying for a while, but God does not seem to be doing anything. Problems that we know God can answer, but we're not sure if He will. What can we do?

The father brought his son to the disciples, but they could not help him. Man can let us down and disappoint us, but if we set our hope and confidence in the Lord, we will not be shaken (Psalm 62:5–6).

It's the cry from the heart of a father for his beloved son. When we've tried everything possible, no doctors, no counseling, nothing works. The battle is so intense that we are drained and worn out, while the enemy is relentless in attacking in more vicious ways, that our faith to believe is now hanging by a thread. Come to Jesus. Jesus alone has the power to rebuke that demonic spirit to set our loved ones and us free from every stronghold.

And Jesus is still saying today that all things are possible to one who believes.

He Dropped His Blanket

Jesus stood still, and said, "Call him."

Mark 10:49 (WEB)

We meet blind Bartimaeus in Mark 10:46–52. In the biblical days, there was no way of supporting oneself financially if a person was blind except to beg. And Bartimaeus was one of them. He had a special cloak that he carried wherever he went to keep him warm in the cold weather and as a blanket at night. It was his most prized possession.

There's something different about the passersby today. Bartimaeus sensed the hurried footsteps and heard that Jesus was coming his way. He understood who Jesus is, and he wanted something greater for himself. He shouted and called on Jesus. But the crowd told Bartimaeus to keep quiet, but he shouted even louder until Jesus told his disciples to "Call him." God always hears us even through the loud noise around us, so don't allow others to discourage us from coming to God.

As soon as Jesus called for Bartimaeus, he immediately threw his coat, jumped up, and approached Jesus. Bartimaeus received his miracle before the miracle happened. It was at that moment that he threw off his old garment and his old identity as a blind beggar. He let go of the most important thing in his life. He leaped in faith for his new vision.

Then Jesus asked him, "What do you want Me to do for you?" It was obvious, so why did Jesus ask? Jesus must have had a reason.

The story of blind Bartimaeus also opens our eyes to spiritual blindness. Sometimes we can get so accustomed to our limitations. Our regrets and disappointments can shift our focus. The pain of our circumstances can blind us so that we run to the wrong places for answers. Jesus is asking, are we willing to change and have a new perspective?

"Lord, I want to see"—Bartimaeus had to verbalize his desire to see things in a new way. There is a difference between knowing the facts and knowing the truth. The fact was that he was blind, but the truth is that nothing is impossible with God.

Jesus told him: "Go your way. Your faith has healed you" (Mark 10:52, NKJV):

- faith to cry out for mercy,
- faith to ignore the negative oppositions to call on God,
- faith to believe and let go of the past,
- faith to let go of the most valuable possession for God.

Where he once lived in darkness, Jesus has now given him light. He no longer needed the cloak that defined who he was. Nothing that the world could offer mattered anymore. He found something greater and moved on with a new identity of following Christ.

Jesus is still asking us, "What do you want Me to do for you?" Are we willing to change? Let us step out in faith for a 20/20 vision and see things in a way we have never seen before.

Your Prayer Has Been Heard

*But they had no child, because Elizabeth was barren,
and they both were well advanced in years.*

Luke 1:7 (WEB)

Did you ever feel as if God may have forgotten you?

In Luke 1:5-24, we meet a priest named Zechariah and his wife, Elizabeth. They had no children and were well past their childbearing age. It was time for Zechariah to minister in the temple, and while he was performing his priestly duties, an angel named Gabriel appeared. Zechariah was taken by surprise that he was shaken in fear, so the angel said, "Do not be afraid. Your prayer has been heard; and your wife Elizabeth will bear a son and you shall call his name John" (Luke 1:13, HCSB).

Zechariah and Elizabeth may have prayed passionately for a child but gave up and stopped believing that God would answer their prayer. Maybe they were not meant to have a child. So, God sent the angel to tell them that He did not forget them.

What have you been praying for? Some of us have been praying for health, relationship, or financial breakthroughs but with each passing year that nothing has happened that we begin to accept that if it did not happen sooner, it is likely never going to happen. We hide our disappointment with the resignation that this is God's will.

Zachariah asked how this could be possible. He was being realistic of their physical limitations and focused on the natural contrary to his spiritual life of fully serving God. We probably do not realize how much we can be like Zechariah and that our situation is never going to change, so we become skeptical not because we don't want to believe but because we are afraid to be disappointed.

Is anything too hard for God? We may not always know what God is doing behind the scenes, and though things may seem impossible in the natural world, one word from God can turn that impossible dream to come alive.

Zechariah had good news to share, but because of unbelief during that angelic visitation, he lost his voice. Often, time spent in solitude with God brings a new perspective and meaning. So, we are to be careful with our words not to cancel God's promises. Yet, with God's grace, Zechariah received the promise and healing. Let this be our lesson not to sabotage our blessing with unbelief. Instead, dream with God. "For the eyes of the Lord are over the righteous, and his ears are open unto their prayers" (1 Peter 3:12, KJV).

Let our hearts be open to receiving our miracle today.

Let It Be According to Your Word

Confused and disturbed,
Mary tried to think what the angel could mean.

Luke 1:29 (NLT)

We meet Mary in Luke 1:26–38—a young teenage girl engaged to Joseph. Joseph and Mary were not celebrities in their time. And like any young bride-to-be, Mary must have been planning her wedding and the new life she would have with Joseph.

Then God sent His messenger angel Gabriel to speak to Mary that she has found favor with the Lord, and she will conceive and give birth to a son, and she will name Him Jesus. But Mary was bothered and confused. How was this possible knowing she was a virgin?

And the angel said, "The Holy Spirit will come on you, and the power of the Most High will overshadow you. Therefore also the holy one who is born from you will be called the Son of God" (Luke 1:35, WEB).

Mary said, "Behold, the servant of the Lord; let it be done to me according to your word" (Luke 1:38, WEB).

The course of Mary's life was reordered, and she had to take on a new role in God's purpose beyond her own. How was this going to affect her engagement to Joseph? What about her family? She was concerned, yet she did not consider the consequences involved. She had the courage to trust in God's word and His plan. She may not have fully grasped God's bigger purpose with many unanswered questions, yet she responded and accepted her new role and surrendered her life and her baby to God's will. Her destiny was changed, and the future of all humanity was forever changed with God's greatest gift of love.

We may never know for sure why God chose Mary, but the Lord does not see things the way we do. Man tends to look at the outside appearance, but God looks at the heart.

Sometimes God's plans for our lives may be different from what we planned. If God were to ask us to do something, what would our answer be? We can't see through the thick clouds surrounding us. We look at how big the world is, and we focus on how small we are, our weaknesses, our lack of training or experience, and our lack of connections. Mary didn't worry about the details but simply trusted that God was aware of her situation. God is also aware of our situation, and we can ask questions when we don't understand, but with God, nothing is impossible. All He wants is our heart, a willing heart.

So, when God calls, will we be willing? Will we trust God's word and respond to that call and submit to the assignment He has for us? Will we go on that journey and say, "Lord, I will walk with You to the unknown, through the road, maybe one I have not gone before."

And say, "I am Your servant. Let Your will be done through me."

The Shepherds Came

*There were shepherds in the same country staying in
the field, and keeping watch by night over their flock.
Behold, an angel of the Lord stood by them, and the
glory of the Lord shone around them,
and they were terrified.*

Luke 2:8–9 (WEB)

The illustration and lesson of the shepherds may not be as relevant in today's modern world, but the story about the shepherds gives us some foundation for the kind of relationship God is establishing with humanity.

A shepherd can be rough and dirty mostly because he is out in the fields day and night to take care of and watch over his sheep. He knows each one of his sheep, and when a predator comes, a shepherd armed only with a rod and slingshot fights a wolf, a bear, or a lion. A shepherd's love, sacrifice, and commitment to his sheep is a demonstration of God's love for his people.

The shepherds were sitting in that dark, cold, and lonely space with the dangers of the night threatening their sheep when suddenly, the night sky was opened with an explosion of light as the angel appeared, and the stillness was broken by the loud voice speaking directly to them. They were terrified, but the angel reassured them:

Fear not: for, behold, I bring you good tidings of great joy, which shall be to all people. For unto you is born this day in the city of David a Saviour, which is Christ the Lord. And this shall be a sign unto you; Ye shall find the babe wrapped in swaddling clothes, lying in a manger.

Luke 2:9–14 (KJV)

These lowly shepherds were tending sheep for the Passover sacrifice. They were the first to receive the message that the sacrifice of lambs would soon end. Jesus, the Lamb of God, has come to be the perfect sacrifice for the sins of all people. This was not only an ending of an era but the beginning of a time that would change the world forever.

And the shepherds said to each other, "Let's go to Bethlehem, now, and see this thing that has happened, which the Lord has made known to us" (Luke 2:15, WEB).

What about the sheep? Who would watch over them if they left to see what the angel said? The shepherds did not have to form a committee to decide a plan of action. They did not say, "Let's think about it. Now, who is going to watch the sheep while some of us go to verify what the angel just said?" The shepherds immediately left everything to be with Jesus, the perfect Lamb of God.

We are also invited to come and join the symphony of angels praising God and saying, "Glory to God in the highest, on earth peace, good will toward men" (Luke 2:14, WEB).

When You Have Crazy Friends

Seeing their faith, he said to him, "
Man, your sins are forgiven you."

Luke 5:20 (WEB)

The story goes in Luke 5:17–39 that Jesus was back in Capernaum. News traveled fast that Jesus was teaching in someone's house. Many religious leaders also came to attend, so it was crowded. And the presence of God's healing power came in that meeting.

Four men wanted to bring their paralyzed friend to Jesus for healing. He was totally helpless—no wheelchair then or any modern conveniences and no way to earn his living. It was a standing room only, and they could not get him through the door. These men believed that, if they could only bring him to Jesus—but there simply was no way. Yet they were determined. One of them came up with a crazy idea of taking him down from the roof. And these four friends wasted no time, so, with bare hands and whatever they could grab, they worked to rip and make a hole in the roof. The crowd heard the banging as debris and dirt were falling on their heads. Some light started to come through the hole and hit the floor.

Wondering, they looked up and down through the hole, and a man was lowered directly into where Jesus was standing.

Jesus, seeing the man, said, "Friend, your sins are forgiven." His friends, who were up on the roof, may have asked, "What did Jesus say?" It was obvious that he needed physical healing. Others in the room may have said, "This poor man was beyond any medical breakthrough, so he needed financial help."

Friends, we may have family or friends who don't know Jesus. They may be going through difficult or traumatic times that they are not able to pull themselves out of the trouble they are in. They become paralyzed to the degree that they are incapable of doing even the basic things in life. We often see them as helpless and perceive that they need better education, financial assistance, or emotional help. We need to see beyond the natural and ask God to let us see through His eyes of love, grace, and mercy. God alone has the authority to forgive sins, but God always places watchmen to stand in the gap for those who are helpless. He wants to heal the sick, give hope to the hopeless, and restore life to the dying.

Disappointments can happen when every possible door seems closed. We do not have to struggle alone. This paralyzed man may not have enough faith or hope of getting better. But these four friends did the unthinkable because they truly cared and were determined, believing that if they could only bring him to Jesus, he would be healed. Faith with faithful action. God can give us creative ways to reach out to the most impossible person or situation. Get out of the box and let creativity flow to find that door that gives us access to make the impossible possible.

There is a door that leads to freedom. It's the door of Jesus that leads to life and blessings as God destined for our loved ones. Don't give up.

Outside Appearance

He called his disciples, and from them he chose twelve, whom he also named apostles.

Luke 6:13 (WEB)

Luke 6:16 listed the names of the disciples who became the apostles of Jesus. Out of the twelve, only with the name Judas Iscariot was added a description as one "who became a traitor."

For three years, Judas Iscariot was a dedicated follower of Jesus. He learned and experienced the power of walking with Jesus to heal the sick, cast out demons, cleanse lepers, and move in signs, wonders, and miracles. But he had a weakness for his love for money. He was appointed treasurer, but he was a thief and took money from the box (John 12:6). Jesus knew but did not openly rebuke him. And none of Judas's fellow disciples suspected his dishonesty. Judas was fully aware of the sinful thing he was doing, but his love for money was stronger.

Outside appearances can be deceiving. Judas started as a thief to become a traitor and finally took his own life.

We learn from the beginning about Judas's weakness. We also read that Judas betrayed Jesus when Satan entered him (Luke 22:3, WEB). We also have weaknesses, and Satan will use that weakness to deceive a follower of God.

Is there a lifestyle with a secret sin? One can say, "God knows I'm working on it." What starts as something minor could easily lead to destruction. Satan only comes in and sets up camp in our life when we open the door of sin. A small unconfessed sin is a doorway to a big disaster. We say, "God will give me strength to overcome." Yes, but is there repentance?

Judas felt sorry and tried to return the money he was paid for his betrayal. But being sorry is not the same as being repentant. Repentance brings not only a change of mind but the realization of the sin committed against God and turning toward God for undeserved forgiveness.

Judas's life serves as a warning in various ways. Others may see that outward appearance of goodness and piety, but God sees right through our hearts. Yet God is ever patient to give us chances to come and humble ourselves before the Lord. When we come before God with a repentant heart, He is faithful to forgive and wipe our slate clean.

Looking Out on That Road

But while he was still far off, his father saw him,
and was moved with compassion,
and ran, and fell on his neck, and kissed him.

Luke 15:20 (WEB)

The parable of the prodigal son in Luke 15:11–32 is often read with the lessons for the errant son, but today, let's look at the story from the heart of the father.

In the parable, the father was a wealthy landowner. It was customary for sons to help and manage the family property, but the younger son asked his father to give him his share of the inheritance. The parable did not explain why the son wanted to leave, but we know that he wanted to be independent and live an exciting, extravagant lifestyle. From the cultural perspective, to ask for one's share of inheritance while the father was still alive was considered unthinkable and shameful behavior, not only to him but to the family. It was as if he could not wait for his father to die to receive his share of his father's estate. The relationship between the father and son was broken in humiliation and shame. The father could have denied his request, but he granted it.

We can be in the story.

Are we going through a painful struggle in our relationship with a loved one, whether it's a spouse, a child, or a family member? Someone we love has done the unthinkable to go after the ways of the world. That loved one who seeks fulfillment after the pleasures of the world that can never truly satisfy. We start to wonder if our prayers are going to be answered. Each day, we battle with sadness and emptiness inside if we will ever see our loved one turn around. This season may seem endless with no hope in sight, but we can't give up for the sake of our loved one. God sees the lies, the deception, the wrong relationships. He said, "I have seen his ways, and will heal him. I will lead him also, and restore comforts to him…" (Isaiah 57:18, WEB). This is God's promise to you and me.

The father did not stop the son from leaving, but he never stopped loving him. Day after day, he would look toward that road hoping to see his son's familiar stride. It did not take long, and the prodigal son lost all his money with his wild lifestyle. When he saw how the pigs had better food than him, he decided to return, humble himself, and beg his father for work as a servant. But the father, through the dusty fields, saw from a distance as the familiar figure slowly came into focus. Overcome with joy, the father ran to meet, embrace, and kiss his son. He immediately told the servants to give him the best robe and a ring and prepare a feast to celebrate his return. Amazing grace.

We, too, have a forgiving Father who not only welcomes every wayward child back but restores lost resources, opportunities, and relationships.

It's the season of believing God for restoration. Our season of waiting will soon end. There will be healing and restoration of that broken relationship. Just as we long for our loved one to return, our heavenly Father is looking out on that road with a robe, a ring, and a great feast to welcome His beloved home.

The Road to Jericho

*For the Son of Man came to seek and
to save that which was lost.*

Luke 19:10 (WEB)

We meet Zaccheus, a rich man, in Luke 19:1–10. Zaccheus was a chief tax collector, and when he heard that Jesus was passing through Jericho, he wanted to see Him. But wherever Jesus went, a crowd followed Him.

The Sycamore Tree. He was short in height with an enormous heart for Jesus. He could not see beyond the crowd, but that did not discourage or stop him. Seeing the impressive height and spread of the Sycamore tree, he ran ahead and climbed the tree to rise above the crowd for a clear vision of Jesus. Our weaknesses and limitations are not reasons enough to stop us from coming to Jesus. There is a Sycamore tree for you and me.

The Crowd. Zaccheus had the position and wealth, but the world despised him. He was aware of his reputation, yet Zaccheus was determined not to be deterred by the crowd. He may have looked ridiculous sitting on the tree, but he did not care. He was determined to see Jesus.

We, too, may have limitations and challenges that can hinder us from having a personal encounter and deeper relationship with God. But the crowd is not the problem.

When Jesus reached the Sycamore tree, He stopped, looked up, and said, "Zacchaeus, hurry and come down, for today I must stay at your house" (Luke 19:5, WEB). They had never met before, but Jesus stopped and called him by his name as if He knew Zacchaeus as a friend. And Jesus invited Himself to go to Zaccheus's house. According to the custom then, to be a guest in his house meant Jesus would spend time and share a meal with him and his family.

Jesus always knocks at our door and will come to the homes of those who open their hearts to His presence.

Everyone saw and heard Jesus, and they began to complain and grumble, "Why would Jesus go and be the guest to this crook? Why would Jesus choose to associate with a man like Zaccheus?" The disciples could have wondered, "Jesus, what are You thinking?"

The crowd saw the sinner, but Jesus saw his heart and drew him to Himself.

With that one encounter with Jesus, Zaccheus confessed and repented his sins and offered restitution to those he had wronged. Salvation came to him and his family.

The road from Jericho to Jerusalem was a dangerous and difficult one, but Jesus dared to go to meet Zaccheus. He will also walk through the dusty streets to find you and me.

God's love transcends our understanding. He will search for us in the unlikeliest place, for Jesus came to find and give life to those who are lost and dying. All He asks is a repentant heart and the faith to believe.

If You Only Knew

"How is it that you, being a Jew,
ask for a drink from me, a Samaritan woman?"
(For Jews have no dealings with Samaritans.)

John 4:9 (WEB)

In John 4, we meet a nameless Samaritan woman who came to the well day after day when no one else was there. She avoided meeting other women who would gather and socialize in the morning, so her drawing water at midday gives us a hint that she was an outcast, despised not only by other races but by her very own people. She was lonely and isolated, being the talk of the town, living a lifestyle as a woman who had five husbands, and the man she was living with now was not her husband.

One day, Jesus sent the disciples to go and get food while he went to Samaria. He arrived by the well at noon when no one was there. Then the Samaritan woman came to draw water as she usually did. Jesus spoke to her, "Give me a drink" (John 4:7, WEB). Traditionally, a Jewish rabbi would not talk to a woman, above all, a Samaritan woman with a questionable reputation in public. But Jesus did. She was surprised by His friendliness and asked Him why a Jewish man would ask her for a drink. But Jesus continued to engage her in a conversation.

He told her,

> If you knew the gift of God, and who it is who says to you, "Give me a drink," you would have asked him, and he would have given you living water. [...] Everyone who drinks of this water will thirst again, but whoever drinks of the water that I will give him will never thirst again.
>
> John 4:10–14 (WEB)

The woman said, "Sir, give me this water, so that I don't get thirsty, neither come all the way here to draw" (John 4:15, WEB).

Everyone in this town drank the water from this well to quench their natural thirst. But Jesus offered her a drink that satisfies at the deepest level. He conversed with this outcast and revealed Himself to this sinner. When she confessed her sinful life, salvation was hers, and she left her jar just as the disciples arrived.

No one may understand what we are going through because they have not walked where we have. We may be doing things that we do not want to do, and like the Samaritan woman, we want to run from the feeling of shame, so we plan our day to avoid meeting others. But God cares, and He will come and meet us where we are, just like that woman at the well. He values us more than we think.

Jesus sent the disciples away when He met with the woman. God will make a way so that those who are most likely to speak negatively about us will not even be around. For God does not condemn us. He will not embarrass or put us in an awkward position in front of many. He wants us to know how much we are loved. He is right there for us.

The water that the world offers will never truly satisfy, but come and drink the living water that God is offering. And leave that jar behind.

Launch Out into the Deep

Launch out into the deep,
and let down your nets for a draught.

Luke 5:4 (KJV)

Peter and his friends were out fishing all night, and at dawn, they headed back to shore without a single catch. Then Jesus told Peter to go back and launch into the deep, contrary to Peter's training and experience. Peter could have told Him, "Didn't you see we were out all night and caught nothing?" Despite his frustration from the past failure, Peter decided, "Master, we worked all night, and took nothing; but at your word I will let down the net" (Luke 5:5, WEB). When they pulled up their nets, they were amazed by the size of their catch that they had to signal to their fishing partners on the other boat to come and help them. There were so many fish that their boats started to sink—a turnaround from lack to overflowing abundance because they humbled themselves to leave the confines of logic and experience and dared into the outer realms of the unknown at Jesus's words.

What were the odds? Yet, no one of Peter's experienced companions complained. With one man's obedience, they were rewarded with a great catch they had not ever seen before.

With our best training and experience, we strive, work hard, and even lose sleep, but we can still fail. Are we willing to go into the deep and unfamiliar waters? When we launch, we, too, will learn that God accomplishes greater things because of our faith. Faith to activate the impossible.

God also wants to bless us beyond what we have ever experienced or seen before. There is something about obedience that touches the heart of God. When we obey, He will surely bless us and all those who are with us, family and friends, who may not even know the Lord. God's power is greater than our limitations.

Will we trust God for the breakthrough in our lives? Do you hear God saying, "Go back and launch into the deep?" Will we say, like Peter, "Lord, I'm tired, frustrated, and disappointed. I worked all night and had nothing, but at Your word, I will let the net down"?

Expect radical change.

Do You Love Me?

Come and eat breakfast!

John 21:12 (WEB)

It was three years ago when Jesus called the fishermen for a greater call, to be fishers of men. They walked in the supernatural, healing incurable diseases, feeding the 5,000, and calming the stormy seas, but with Jesus's death and resurrection, Peter and the other disciples felt lost and decided to go back to fishing—fish.

We go back to the garden of Gethsemane (Matthew 26:33–35): three times, Peter denied knowing Jesus. Peter could not handle the pressure to hold on to his conviction, and when things went wrong, he denied knowing Jesus. He could no longer continue with the ministry he signed up for and decided to go back to his old lifestyle.

As the sun was rising, Peter and his companions were coming back from fishing all night, but Jesus was already waiting to serve them breakfast. After breakfast, Jesus asked Peter, "Do you love me?" three times (John 21:15–17). Why did Jesus ask Peter the same question three times?

For each time that Peter said, "I don't know this man," on that dark night in Gethsemane, now he was saying to Jesus, "Lord, You know that I love You." Three times, he reversed his broken promises and denials and affirmed his love for Jesus and his willingness to be a fisher of men. Jesus knew Peter's heart, and He knew where Peter would be at this moment. He came to offer forgiveness and reconciliation. It was a new day for Peter and his companions.

Life has many twists and turns, and when things don't happen the way we planned, we get disappointed and discouraged because we don't expect life to look like this. We get anxious, overwhelmed, and weary, feeling as if we're in the middle of nowhere, that we begin to question the path we're taking and even the goodness of God. We feel alone, but it does not mean He abandoned us. God is watching us. We try to assess our possibilities, but we only see the impossibilities. It does not mean God is no longer in it. God is with us. He knows everything, including every setback we will experience. Our impossibility is only the beginning of God's possibilities. He will not allow anything to stop His plans concerning our life. We can't give up. Look to the new day.

Tie Your Loose Ends

Wherefore gird up the loins of your mind, be sober,
and hope to the end for the grace that is to be brought
unto you at the revelation of Jesus Christ...

1 Peter 1:13 (KJV)

In biblical times, men and women wore long flowing clothes like robes. These long robes would get in the way when they do hard work or go into battle. So, they needed to keep them off the ground by gathering the ends of the garment and tucking them into their belt or tying them in a knot. And so, the expression "gird up your loins" means to tie the loose ends and get ready for hard work or battle. Why did Peter depict this picture of girding up the loins of our minds?

Why do we struggle much with our thoughts? In Genesis 3:5, the devil sowed a lie to Eve. The mind is where seeds are sown. The door of the soul is the mind, so what we receive, we become.

Peter is not talking about the clothes we wear but about our minds. He is telling us to deal with the loose ends of our minds and emotions because if we allow wrong thoughts or a wrong tradition, principle, or conviction to influence us, they can slow us down or hinder our walk with God. We will be like the warrior who goes into battle, but his garment hangs loose and stumbles. But we are to secure those loose ends with the Word of God as our belt of *truth*.

Our thoughts are the beginning of everything in our life. Whether we like it or not, our thoughts can dictate the way we live our life. We may have strong personal inclinations that we often say, "This is just the way I am," because we learned to think, act, and behave in a way that becomes a habit pattern from a very young age, maybe to feel accepted or loved. To break this pattern, we need self-restraint. This is only possible when we meditate and allow God's word to renew our minds. God's word is like a powerful sword to cut through our hearts so that our thoughts are transformed for good.

As Peter said, the mind is like a flowing robe that we must exercise control. Each time we change a thought, our life changes also. Change means there's a turning around and going against the old patterns because each time we do something, we either strengthen or weaken it. When we try to resist a temptation, the first time may be difficult, but the next time, it gets better and then easier until we fully overcome it. In a similar way, the first time with sin may be hard, but the more we do it, it becomes easier until it becomes a way of life.

Are there any loose ends in your life? We are warned not to conform to the ways of the world that can lead us into compromise and ultimately away from the path of God. We start with our minds by holding every thought captive (2

Corinthians 10:5) and allowing God's Word to cleanse our minds and emotions. And when troubles and temptations come, we can have divine strength to overcome and say, "I can do all things through Christ, who strengthens me" (Philippians 4:13, WEB).

A Friend in Need

I tell you, although he will not rise and give it to him
because he is his friend, yet because of his persistence,
he will get up and give him as many as he needs.

Luke 11:8 (WEB)

The story in Luke 11:5–8 is part of a series of Jesus's teaching on prayer. Jesus told the story of a villager and a neighbor. In biblical times, hospitality was a vital part that was deeply embedded in that culture.

It was midnight, and everyone was asleep, but a villager was awakened by an unexpected guest who had come from a long journey. Shops were closed for the night, and all through the town, lights were out as neighbors slept. But it would be embarrassing and unwelcoming for the host not to serve a meal to his guest, especially after a long and exhausting journey. He knew which neighbor would have some bread and was compelled to knock and ask for three loaves of bread. But the neighbor told him to go away, "Doesn't he realize it's midnight and the family is sleeping? I have to get up early tomorrow for work."

But the man, who needed bread, kept on knocking. He banged the door louder, saying, "Please, I need some bread for a friend who is hungry." And the neighbor said, "He will keep me awake and disturb everyone in the house unless I give him what he is asking." Finally, he gave him what he asked for, not because he was being a good neighbor or because they were friends, but because this man was shameless, bold, and persistent.

We, too, may have someone in our life who is going through many dark nights of struggles and trials and is too weary from a long journey. Will we be willing to help that friend?

If we don't have what that friend specifically needs, will we be bold and persistent in calling on the one who is able?

Let's not limit God but keep asking until we receive our promised blessings like the persistent friend in our story and like Jacob, who wrestled till dawn and refused to let go until he received his blessing (Genesis 32:26).

The Annoying, Nagging Widow

Will not God grant justice to His elect who cry out to Him day and night? Will He delay to help them?

Luke 18:7 (HCSB)

The story of the persistent widow and the unjust judge in Luke 18:1–8 is an example of the power of prayer and never giving up. Losing her loved one was already hard, and trying to put the pieces of her life together, was even more difficult when an adversary came against her. We don't know the details. Was it something against her husband that she had no knowledge of? Was it a family member with a financial claim? Was it after her land? She had every reason to feel sorry for herself, but she did not lean on her weakness and vulnerability to rely on her family and friends. And she refused to confront her adversary. But she was convinced of her right and sought legal protection from the higher authority. The judge who handled her case was unjust and didn't fear God, nor did he have any compassion for the people. Although her case was already in progress in court, she went after the judge, pleading for justice. For a while, he kept ignoring her, but he realized that this woman would not stop nagging and annoying him unless he gave her justice. But God is not like the judge.

We, too, can face an adversary that comes against our health, relationships, or finances. And like the widow, we don't always receive an immediate answer to prayer. How long do we have to wait for our prayers to be answered? A delay does not mean denial, but we need to deal with the situation. What God said He will do, He will do it. We can't give up but remind ourselves of the infallibility of God's word and gain strength to steady our faith to believe and trust God's perfect timing. So, "let us therefore come boldly unto the throne of grace, that we may obtain mercy, and find grace to help in time of need" (Hebrews 4:16, KJV).

God is always watching to change the hearts of even the hard-hearted on our behalf. And so, we have hope because God not only sees and hears our cries, but He answers.

Things Would Have Been Different

Jesus said to her, "Didn't I tell you that if you believed, you would see God's glory?"

John 11:40 (WEB)

In the book of John 11, we read about the village of Bethany, where the sisters Martha and Mary lived with their brother Lazarus. Lazarus became ill, and both Martha and Mary immediately sent word to Jesus, but He did not come until four days after Lazarus died. Today's story is about Martha's encounter with Jesus.

When Martha heard that Jesus was coming, she immediately went out to meet Him. Martha said, "Lord, if you would have been here, my brother wouldn't have died" (John 11:21, WEB).

Martha spoke with a tone of disappointment. She was saying, "Why did You take so long to come? You could have done something, and Lazarus would still be alive today." Jesus healed many others before, and He could have healed her brother too. Despite the disappointment, Martha expressed some hope for a miracle, so she said, "Even now I know that whatever you ask of God, God will give you" (John 11:22, WEB).

Faith!

Jesus answered that her brother would live again (verse 23). Then Jesus told her, "I am the resurrection and the life. He who believes in me will still live, even if he dies." Then Jesus asked, "Do you believe this?" (John 11:25–26, WEB). She quickly answered yes and went home to tell her sister that Jesus was there.

Martha believed in the promise of the future. Yes, she knew that her brother would live again on the last day. This was what she learned and believed according to the teachings she grew up with. This conversation was fading her hope for the sign and the wonder of that which she was hoping to see today. Did Martha begin to doubt, or simply did she not understand what Jesus was trying to tell her?

We, too, can experience troubles and disappointments. We can get distracted when we hear many voices that confuse us and heighten our pain, disappointment, and sorrow that we begin to doubt and question our relationship with God. If only God answered our prayer, things would have been different.

But God knows and hears our cries, and He comes to comfort us. He will not rebuke us but challenge us to defy our knowledge and understanding of the natural world concerning anything about life and what matters to us.

He may be challenging our faith to believe that today can be our day to receive a miracle. Nothing is too hard for

God. And for every difficult and hopeless circumstance, for that miracle we have been praying for, He is able. It's not too late, but today may be the day He will turn things around to demonstrate His power and glory.

Simply believe!

If He Only Came Sooner

When therefore he heard that he was sick,
he stayed two days in the place where he was.

John 11:6 (WEB)

We continue about the sisters Martha and Mary and their brother Lazarus in John 11:32–43 (WEB). This story is about Mary. Many came to comfort the family, but when Martha told Mary that Jesus was on His way and asking for her, she immediately left those who came to console her to find comfort in Jesus. And they also left to follow her. When she saw Jesus, she fell at His feet, saying, "Lord, if you would have been here, my brother wouldn't have died" (John 11:32, WEB).

When Jesus saw her weeping and the others who were with her weeping also, He groaned in the spirit. He was so troubled, moved, and wept.

When they saw Him weeping, they said to each other how He loved Lazarus and that if only He had come sooner, He could have healed him, and their beloved would still be alive.

But Jesus already knew that the end result would be to the glory of God, not death.

We, too, can go through situations where we don't understand why God seems silent to our cries and prayers. We hope for the impossible and find ourselves asking, "Why,

God? If only You had been here with me in my most difficult time, things would have been different." We get into mixed emotions of one moment believing for the best and the next feeling disillusioned, disappointed, and though we may not want to admit some regret that things are not the way we wanted.

When we don't receive an immediate answer to our prayer, we wonder if God has forgotten us, but His silence or the delays do not necessarily mean denial. Sometimes our battle looks like a defeat. Victory from our perspective is often different from God's perspective. We say, "God, I'm dying," but God says, "This sickness is not unto death." Even when God seems far away and out of reach, we must trust His timing. In His perfect timing, He may be setting us up for a miracle that He may be glorified through us.

Let us continue to posture ourselves in humility as Mary bowed before His presence.

So, Jesus went to the tomb and shouted, "Lazarus, come out" (John 11:43, WEB).

God will do the same for you and me today. He is the giver of life, and He loves and cares for our loved ones and us. He feels our deepest pain and sorrows, and He comforts us. Everything that is lost and long gone in our lives, even death, is not stronger than God. It's okay if we don't understand everything that happens to us, but we can run to God for comfort so that we can dream again and live again.

Healing in Forgiveness

But if ye forgive not men their trespasses,
neither will your Father forgive your trespasses.

Matthew 6:14–15 (KJV)

In life, we can go through peaks and valleys. Each has a way of directly affecting our actions. But when we're in the valley, we could experience devastating times that we don't know how to move on without the grace and healing that only God can give.

Perhaps you were betrayed, or a friendship ended, or someone did something that really hurt you, and you don't understand why. It may not be because of you. There's anger and even attempts to hide the pain with hopes that eventually, time will heal. We can walk into places, hear a word that holds painful memories, and we relive the pain. Unresolved emotional hurt robs us of peace. It leads to bitterness that even causes physical illness that doctors may not be able to cure.

We cannot control others, and sometimes, we cannot forget the things that happened in our lives, but we can take charge of our thoughts and our emotions not to allow those events to become excuses that we are nothing but a victim of circumstances. God wants to get us through our most difficult times.

When we trust God and hold onto His promise, the more deeply He heals us. God is closer than we think. "The Lord is near the brokenhearted; He saves those crushed in spirit" (Psalm 34:18, HCSB).

When we can't get past the hurt and the anger, it's best to give it to God. David wrote in Psalm 51:17 that the sacrifice we can offer God is a broken spirit. He will not reject a broken and repentant heart. God is our healer, but there's one thing He tells us to do:

Forgive. This is a command.

God wants us to release, let go, and leave everything with Him.

Forgiving can be one of the hardest things that God asks us, but He also knows we cannot do it on our own. Healing of wounds requires a deliberate effort to forgive. It is a process, but as we lay down every burden that we have been holding in our hearts to God, He fills us with a love so powerful that it breaks through everything that brings healing and redemption. All to prepare us for the greater things that God has already planned for us.

It is time to let go of the past. Move on. With God's grace, we can choose to forgive as many times as necessary while God heals us. The reward is worth it.

On the Third Day

But Mary was standing outside at the tomb weeping.

John 20:11 (WEB)

In that dark hour before the break of dawn, Mary went to the tomb and, through a faint light, saw it was open and empty. Then suddenly, two angels in dazzling clothes appeared. The angel asked, "Why do you seek the living among the dead? For He is not here but is risen!" (Luke 24:4–8, WEB). She was unaffected and oblivious to her angelic encounter. Nothing else mattered but the anguish and the pain of yesterday. It's hard to hope when we feel hopeless and the world around us is dark.

How long are you going to mourn over that relationship? You may be brokenhearted; perhaps you lost a loved one, or you received a negative report, or your dreams have been shattered. Fixating on past mistakes, failures, lost relationships, or missed opportunities will get us trapped in the past and buried in the graveyard of hopelessness and despair.

Jesus came and spoke to Mary, but she thought He was the gardener until He called her name. Then she turned around to face Him.

God is with us, but we must be cognizant of God's presence. He is with us to help us get through. It's hard to gather the strength to fight for things to get better. We all need God's grace. We all need a fresh start. But we must decide to do whatever needs to be done to move on and walk into the future in God's promise.

It was on the third day. Death overpowers the world, and it is the last thing in the world, but God's love is stronger. And that empty tomb is a proclamation that God did not forsake Jesus. Jesus conquered death so that we, too, can prevail over our every circumstance. It was prophesied years ago. It was a promise that many have long forgotten. And when we have a promise from God, it doesn't matter how dark the night is; nothing, not even death, can stop His word. What God says He will do, He will do it. Whatever you think is lost and gone forever—look to the promise. It never fails but will come alive in our darkest time. "Weeping may endure for a night, but joy cometh in the morning" (Psalm 39:5, KJV).

Stay the Course

Simon Peter said to them, "I'm going fishing."
They told him, "We are also coming with you."

John 21:3 (WEB)

A man named Simon had a profitable fishing business. One ordinary day, he met Jesus, and that stirred into his heart the realization of himself, including his weaknesses. He became fully persuaded to let go of everything for a deeper call. He gave it all for what he believed was the greater call of his life—to follow Jesus (Luke 5:1–11).

Simon had no education and no other work experience except fishing. He was rough yet outspoken and strong-willed, with great survival skills from his experience working at sea and in the marketplace.

Simon, the fisherman, became Peter, the fisher of men. For the next three years, Peter went into full-time training. He listened to Jesus's teachings and witnessed miracles of healing. He was dedicated to being the disciple as Jesus taught them. But in many instances, Peter failed. And rather than stepping into the call on his life to be an apostle, Peter returned to his old ways—fishing for fish instead of men (John 21:3). He also took the other disciples with him.

In our own walk with the Lord, we, too, may go through challenges that bring doubt, fear, and uncertainty about our future. We cannot see past the present circumstances of where we are. It's hard to be hopeful about the future when everything we worked for has failed. Like Peter, we feel that after all these years, we failed and that maybe it would be best to cut our losses and get back to where we are more comfortable.

It's hard to stay positive when we have disappointments, but we need to be determined to press through and not walk away when we encounter resistance. Failure can't define us. Our true identity is in the Lord. Our hope is in who we are in God. Sometimes, we don't realize our own strength until we are faced with resistance. But God is with us to teach us to walk by faith and trust Him. God does not set us up to fail. We have the promise that He will never leave us nor forsake us. That is our confidence to get back up, go forward, hope again, dream again, and live again.

With God, we can stay the course and make it through.

Random Chance

But an angel of the Lord spoke to Philip, saying,
Arise, and go toward the south to the way
that goes down from Jerusalem to Gaza.

Acts 8:26 (WEB)

Did you ever wonder if some of the things that happened were mere coincidences or divine setups to usher you into a higher call?

In Acts 8:26–40, we learn about an influential man holding a high position in his government, but according to the law, he was among those to be excluded from worship in the temple (Deuteronomy 23:1). The Ethiopian eunuch knew he was different. He knew that he would never be allowed to participate fully in temple worship because of who he was, but he had a deep desire to know God in a real and personal way, so he traveled this long journey to worship in Jerusalem.

Meanwhile, Philip was preaching in Samaria when an angel told him to go down south. There was no one on that desert road, but Philip went as told. While Philip was walking, the Ethiopian eunuch on his chariot was passing by. God orchestrated this divine setup through a random chance. So, when Philip heard the man reading from the book of Isaiah, he asked if he understood what he was reading. The man answered, "How can I, unless someone explains it to me?" (Acts 8:31, WEB). He invited Philip to ride with him, and right there, the Ethiopian eunuch claimed the promise of God and asked to be baptized.

We could be doing something very important, but sometimes we get interrupted. We don't fully understand why, but our obedience can make a difference in someone's life. Random things that happen may not always make sense, but God knows what lies ahead. If Philip did not go as he was led, things would have been totally different. If we are not sensitive to the movement of God, we will miss the opportunity to speak to someone's life.

The Ethiopian eunuch can be the worst of sinners, an outcast, unworthy, but there is no one beyond God's love and redemption, and God will also send someone on that desert road. We don't really know what's in someone's heart, sometimes even our own heart. But God sees our hearts and motives. As it is written:

> Do not let the son of the foreigner Who has joined himself to the Lord Speak, saying, "The Lord has utterly separated me from His people"; Nor let the eunuch say, "Here I am, a dry tree." For thus says the Lord: "To the eunuchs who keep My Sabbaths, And choose what pleases Me, And hold fast My covenant, Even to them I will give in My house And within My walls a place and a name Better than that

of sons and daughters; I will give them an
everlasting name That shall not be cut off."

Isaiah 56:3–5 (NKJV)

God loves even those that the world considers misfits.
May we have God's eyes and heart to love even the unlovable!

The Road to Damascus

I am Jesus, whom you are persecuting...

Acts 9:5 (WEB)

The story in the book of Acts 9 was about Saul of Tarsus, the overzealous Pharisee who became Paul. He was highly educated, intelligent, and knowledgeable about religious law, culture, and tradition. He was highly driven with great conviction and loyal to his religion. He violently persecuted the followers of Jesus like a vicious wolf who ravaged anyone who opposed the doctrine he believed. On his way to Damascus, a sudden blazing light blinded him, and he fell off his horse and heard Jesus saying, "Saul, Saul, why do you persecute me?" And Saul asked, "Who are you, Lord?" (Acts 9:4:5 WEB). Then Paul was led to go to Straight Street in Damascus. For the next three days, Paul wrestled with everything that he believed, and his sight was restored when he learned the truth about Jesus.

Saul's intention was well in believing that he was doing the right thing for the God he knew until his Damascus encounter led him to the straight path that changed his life forever. God used the very same passion and ferocious focus in him to show God's saving grace to the undeserving and hopeless. And he became the author of many New Testament books in the Bible because of that one encounter in Damascus. And the remarkable story of Paul still happens today, for God will come after that one who is pursuing the wrong things of the world and make that person completely new with a renewed heart on fire for the Lord.

Are you praying for your breakthrough, a prodigal spouse, or a wayward child to come home? Some are saying, "There is no way." Don't give up. There is nothing too hard for God. Though our loved ones and we may be convinced that the lifestyle we chose is right in our eyes and in the world, God can intercept and shed light to expose what is hidden in darkness and reveal the truth.

Today, there is a road to Damascus that leads to the straight path to that one whom God is calling. Like Paul, who changed the course of his journey and became the greatest missionary in the history of the church, we never know when a loved one or we go on that road, and God uses unexpected circumstances to get us off the path that we're on to get us into new possibilities to the greater purpose He has for us.

Open the Gate

*So Peter was kept in prison, but prayer was being
made earnestly to God for him by the church.*

Acts 12:5 (HCSB)

Acts 12:1–19 (WEB) talks about having faith to believe
that our prayers are answered even as we are still praying.

There was growing political and social persecution of
the early church. Herod wanted to kill James and Peter.
They had already lost James, and so the church came
together to earnestly pray on Peter's behalf. So, God sent
an angel to rescue Peter from prison. It was just as Isaiah
prophesied, "And it shall come to pass, that before they call,
I will answer; and while they are yet speaking, I will hear"
(Isaiah 65:24, KJV).

Peter knew that he would be put to death in a few hours,
but that night, while Peter was in his prison cell, heavily
guarded, bound in chains, he was at peace and slept. Then an
angel woke Peter, saying, "Stand up quickly," and immediately,
the chains fell off his hands. Peter thought he was dreaming
or that he had a vision. Then the angel told him, "Get ready
and put on your sandals. Put on your coat and follow me."
Peter followed the angel, and when they reached the iron
gate leading into the city, it opened by itself, so they walked
out into the street. And the angel left. Only then did Peter

realize that this was not a dream or a vision. This can only be the Lord sending an angel to rescue him from the hands of Herod. Peter had to think fast. He had just broken out of prison and had to get off the street, so he headed to Mary's house, where they usually gather in prayer. Peter knocked at the door of the gate, and a servant girl named Rhoda came to answer. She recognized Peter and was overjoyed to see him, but she took off to tell the others, leaving Peter outside the gate. Peter must have been saying, "No, no, no. Let me in." And when Rhoda told them that Peter was here, they were skeptical and told her she was out of her mind, while others said she might have seen an angel.

And so, this incredible story presents a challenge to us. These believers were faithful and prayed earnestly, wholeheartedly for a miracle, yet they had little expectation of God. How many of us are like them or like Rhoda? How many times did we pray fervent prayers but not really believe that our prayer would be answered? Maybe God already answered, yet we continue to pray for the very same concern because we are skeptical.

This is not just their story. We can't pray just to go through the motions, but we must believe that God hears us. We will encounter resistance and obstacles, but God will not leave us alone to grope and fight our way through. He will make a way or send an angel to lead us out of harm's way (Psalm 91:11).

If God promised, we must believe that He will do as He

promised. When we remind Him of His promise, He must answer (1 John 5:14–15) because He said He will. That is our God, and our confidence is in Him alone.

And All They Did Was Praise

Suddenly there was a great earthquake,
so that the foundations of the prison were shaken;
and immediately all the doors were opened and
everyone's chains were loosed.

Acts 16:26 (NKJV)

Our story is in Acts 16:22–34. It's midnight. Paul and Silas were flogged and beaten with rods and then thrown into a cold and dark prison for preaching the gospel. Yet they did not moan and groan, longing for a warm and comfortable bed; they were praying and singing hymns to God. It is easy to pray and sing praises in pleasant times, but this was probably the last thing they wanted to do. Yet they did.

The prisoners in the adjoining cells were wide awake, listening. It was already midnight, yet no one slept or complained, but they listened as Paul and Silas sang of the goodness of God. There was something about their singing hymns to God—sounds prisoners had never heard before— yet the haunting sounds of fear and despair in that cold and dark prison were broken. There was a sense of comfort and new expectation even in the hearts of the toughest men.

The sounds of praise did not only touch Paul, Silas, and the prisoners but moved the heart of God. Suddenly, the ground began to shake, and the prison foundations began to crack. They heard the sound of jangling chains and squeaking as cell doors were opening. Every prisoner realized that his chains had come off.

The guard ran to check on the prisoners, thinking, "Surely, they escaped." This was indeed a perfect opportunity for a prison break, but surprisingly, no one did. The jailer brought Paul and Silas home, and he and everyone in his family received salvation.

We cannot allow opposition and rejection to lock us up in the cage of despair and humiliation so that we wallow in misery with the shackles of despondency. There is a way out. We can choose to praise God and allow His peace to calm the shaking of our emotions. God hears and responds to our prayers and praises in ways beyond our comprehension that even those who are in the "deepest gloom" and imprisoned in the "iron chains of misery" (Psalm 107:10, NLT) will be set free.

And all that Paul and Silas did was praise—because God inhabits the praises of His people (Psalm 22:3).

There is something about our praise that's bigger than us.

It Will Be Just as God Said

*But take courage! None of you will lose your lives,
even though the ship will go down.*

Acts 27:22 (NIV)

It all began when the Lord told Paul, "Paul, you must preach the gospel in Rome" (Acts 23:11), but he was being prevented in ways that no one of us would like to experience.

And the story in Acts 27 continues when Paul, with other prisoners, was to sail to Italy. An experienced traveler after three shipwrecks, he knew how stormy the seas could be at this time of the year, so he advised the centurion and the captain against the timing of this voyage, but they decided to sail on. It was not long after that the weather took a turn for the worst. Turbulent winds blew with crashing waves that violently tossed the boat. For many days there was only darkness as the storm kept raging, battering the ship that passengers feared for their lives and began to lose hope if they would make it through. But the Lord sent an angel to comfort Paul that the ship would be lost, but everyone on board the ship would be saved. So, Paul told the other passengers not to fear. He went on and said, "Cheer up, for

I believe God, that it shall be even as it was told me" (Acts 27:25, KJV). After fourteen days, they ran aground, and the ship was wrecked, but the passengers swam safely to shore.

Why did Paul go through that? Paul was obedient, so we expect God will make it easy for him. But Paul knew the storms in life can be violent and life-threatening, yet he believed that they would all be safe.

We, too, can go through turbulent times. We find ourselves on a journey we did not really choose. There's chaos, confusion, and things happening beyond our control. Rough times in health, relationships, marriage or family, finances.

The moment we receive a promise, we may not realize that seen and unseen things are set into motion. When unforeseen circumstances arise and things don't go as planned, our faith and trust in God are challenged. We get upset and ask, "Did God really say that?" or "What did I do wrong?" Some say, "It's not God's will for me." Others say, "If God really wants me to go, He will make the way easy for me."

But God's ways are higher than ours. When we don't know how life is going to be, God already knows even the worst times in our lives. We cannot allow fear to cripple and deprive us of going places with God. When we take the risk and move away from the security of what we've known, God is faithful to do what He promised. And we can hold on to that promise to be our source of comfort, strength, and courage because it will be just as God said.

The Viper Hidden in the Sticks

But Paul shook the snake off into the fire and suffered no ill effects.

Acts 28:5 (NIV)

In Acts 27–28, we read about Paul and the other prisoners' harrowing experience at sea that wrecked their ship and them finding shelter on an island. The locals welcomed them with kindness and lit a fire to keep them warm. Paul helped keep the fire going, but hidden in the bundle of sticks was a viper. The viper fastened itself to Paul's hand and bit him as the natives watched in horror, expecting Paul to drop dead. But Paul was unperturbed and simply shook it off into the fire and was not harmed. The poison could have ended his life and his mission. But Paul had God's word and promise. No storm, not even death, could stop God's plan or purpose for Paul.

And today, it may be rare for the viper to appear in the physical, but in our daily walk, we can get stung with the venom of betrayal, crafty, cunning, evil behaviors even from those we have a close relationship with—hurtful actions that can wound us deeply. Or someone with crafty words to influence us to lose sight of what we believe is right. Let us be vigilant. Satan has a way of wrapping around our hearts with lies to deceive and blind us. As the snake fastened quickly around Paul's arm, the lies of Satan can easily fasten and weave into our lives. Shake it off quickly, with conviction and determination, and keep that venom from infecting us. It is lethal. We don't always realize how much faith and conviction we have until we come into a situation that makes us dissatisfied and say, "I deserve something better," and get off course, away from the path that God has led us. Or, when we are in that dark place, and false humility is exposed when we say, "This is God's will for me." How quickly we blame God! How soon do we forget that the deadly venom is absorbed and filtering into our system and compelling us to move in that nature. Let's not be deceived. God will not take us this far to abort His plans and leave us wondering what we should do.

The snake had to be exposed. That snake must come out. It cannot remain hidden, or it will sabotage our mission, poison our faith, and destroy us. We must guard our hearts and minds and destroy every defiant attitude, deceptive imagination, and arrogant thinking against the truth of God (2 Corinthians 10:5). Shake it off with your every strength, and let it burn in the fire and give God the glory.

Make Up Your Mind

But let him ask in faith, without any doubting,
for he who doubts is like a wave of the sea,
driven by the wind and tossed.

James 1:6 (WEB)

Are you being torn in two directions? Deep within the heart of a believer is the desire to fully surrender one's life to God, but there is also that strong desire that gives in to self and temptation.

James 1:8 (KJV) says, "A double minded man is unstable in all his ways." That person is inconsistent, can't make up his mind, is unsettled, and has no conviction.

A double-minded man is like having a double heart (Psalm 12:2). That person's loyalty is torn between God and the world, like having a relationship with God and walking with God but may also have a hidden pet sin. That person wants to do the right thing but ends up doing the opposite. Today there is faith, but tomorrow there's a lack of trust. There's spiritual and emotional instability. That's why James 1:22 said that unless we believe and do what we hear from God, we are deceiving ourselves. If we doubt God's ability to answer our prayers, why bother to pray and ask because we will not receive anything we ask?

The opposite of double-mindedness is in Ephesians 6:5. We are to have singleness in our hearts. While most of us deal with some measure of uncertainty and insecurity, we have a difficult time deciding whether there may be certain areas in our minds that make us apprehensive. Such feelings may keep us from taking on certain opportunities. If we are to rise and be successful, we need to address the issue of lack of confidence.

We can remind ourselves that our confidence comes from the Lord. We do not have to know everything about how our life is going to be and how to solve our problems. God does not want us overthinking and worrying about what the future will be. God knows ahead of time, including our fears and the worst things that will happen to us. When we focus on God and His Word, He removes our fears and gives us grace and strength to have His perspective of who we are in a way we have not seen before. Our ability to see things beyond the natural gives us the confidence that God has it all. We can step into our future anchored in God's love and faithfulness to take us to His plans of prosperity and blessings.

The Thoughtful Mind

Finally, brothers, whatever things are true, whatever
things are honorable, whatever things are just, what-
ever things are pure, whatever things are lovely, what-
ever things are of good report: if there is any virtue
and if there is any praise, think about these things.

Philippians 4:8 (WEB)

Paul had no idea that he would preach the very same gospel he intensely fought against. He went from being violent as a ravaging wolf and a persecutor of Christians to completely dedicating his life to serving Jesus Christ, fearless against all opposition.

After his conversion, he spent three years (Galatians 1:18) in prayer and study of the Scriptures before he started his missionary journeys that changed the world. He said, "I am not worthy of being called an apostle after the way I persecuted God's church" (1 Corinthians 15:9, paraphrased). Most likely, the memory of his past was not immediately erased. He may have had remorse or regret when the thought suddenly hit his mind. The explicit details of what happened may have brought anguish.

How can we stop painful memories from haunting us? How can we erase from our minds things that we wish never happened?

A messenger of Satan came to torment Paul (2 Corinthians 12:7). He had to go through an onslaught of mental warfare, like sharp piercing thorns, afflicting him with accusations of his past and of his unworthiness to preach the gospel. He is not alone in this experience. We, too, can face similar attacks.

We, too, have an adversary, the devil, who is a master accuser. He comes into our deep thoughts. Thoughts to make us feel strongly one way that can push us to the limits of our faith in our spiritual walk. We may not be able to stop those thoughts from coming, but we can stop them from lingering.

How do we do it?

It's knowing God's grace and mercy that "if we confess our sins, he is faithful and righteous to forgive us the sins, and to cleanse us from all unrighteousness" (1 John 1:9, WEB).

It's knowing that Satan uses fiery darts of condemnation. It's Satan's weapon to deceive us into thinking that God's forgiveness is no longer available, so God has abandoned us and does not love us. God is against us. But that's a distortion of the truth because Romans 8:1 says there is no condemnation to those who are in Christ Jesus.

So, we need to have a tight rein in our minds by taking undesirable imaginations and evil thoughts to the obedience of Christ (2 Corinthians 10:5). It is hard to train our thoughts to think differently, but when we turn them over to God, He enables us to focus on the right things.

With God, we change our behavior and attitude so that we no longer follow the ways of the world. It all begins with a new mindset (Romans 12:3).

Change of Plans

Was I fickle when I intended to do this?
Or do I make my plans in a worldly manner so that in
the same breath I say both "Yes, yes" and "No, no"?
Do you think I make my plans carelessly?

2 Corinthians 1:17–18 (NIV)

Have you ever been misunderstood, and the more you tried to explain, the worse things turned out? Paul went through that.

Paul stayed in Corinth for eighteen months, where he preached, taught, trained leaders, and started a church. After he left, false teachers came, opposed his leadership, and turned the church against Paul. He planned to visit the church twice but changed his travel plans and ended up visiting them only once. This change in travel plans became an issue. The members were not only disappointed, but it also caused a misunderstanding, and they accused him of being double-minded. In a way, saying he was two-faced, insincere. They jumped to wrong conclusions and criticized his character and integrity.

Paul defended himself, saying that he did not have hidden motives to waver between yes and no. He did not dwell on their false accusations but turned his defense on the trustworthiness of the gospel he preached. For the

283

message of Christ was not a yes today and no tomorrow. He didn't boast of his credentials as an apostle but talked about who he was in God and what God was doing through him (2 Corinthians 1:21–22).

What really happened?

Paul's first visit to Corinth turned out to be troublesome. Corinth was a city of diverse socioeconomic levels with many problems that influenced the Christian converts. Paul had to confront them for their sins, causing a fracture between him and the church. He wanted to heal and restore their relationship, but returning so soon would probably cause more contention, so he sent a letter through Titus to give everyone time to reconsider, work on their unresolved issues, and repent.

Who would have thought that a simple change in plans could bring misunderstanding and cause an attack on Paul's credibility? False accusations that hurt and wound deeply. How do we deal with people like the Corinthians?

When others misunderstand and accuse us, how do we respond? Do we justify our actions and show them our own list of all the wrongs they have done, in spite of us living imperfect lives yet looking for and demanding perfection from everyone else?

The world we are in today is not that different from the Corinthians, and so we learn from Paul that when misunderstandings arise, we strive to live in integrity and sincerity through God's wisdom, understanding, and grace. And if things don't get resolved that quickly, one day, someday, our accusers will fully understand (2 Corinthians 1:13–14).

Physically Present but Mentally Absent

Now when I went to Troas to preach the gospel
of Christ and found that the Lord had opened a door
for me, I still had no peace of mind,
because I did not find my brother Titus there.
So I said goodbye to them and went on to Macedonia.

2 Corinthians 2:12–13 (NIV)

Have you ever been in a gathering, and although you're making remarks, you're not quite engaging in the conversation? You're thinking and worried about someone. You're physically present but mentally absent. You're not alone. Our story in 2 Corinthians 2:12–13 tells us how Paul went through a similar scenario.

When the church in Corinth was infiltrated with false teachings, sexual immorality, division, and confusion, Paul confronted them and wrote a follow-up letter and sent Titus to deliver it personally.

Waiting can be hard. When we call or send a text to our loved ones, we expect an immediate response. If we don't, we worry that something disastrous may have happened. Paul felt the same way, but in biblical times, Paul had to wait for weeks or maybe months for a letter or any news to come.

Then Paul heard from God that he should go to Troas. It seemed like a good opportunity to also meet up with Titus and hear the long-awaited updates about Corinth. But when he arrived in Troas and didn't see Titus, he was perturbed, so he left Troas and went to Macedonia.

What was Paul thinking? Paul obeyed the Lord, so he went to Troas, but he did not have the right mental or emotional frame to preach the gospel and left. This authoritative and powerful man of God was overcome with conflicting emotions. It was not until chapter seven that Paul realized his worrying was needless because God took care of all his concerns.

We can learn from Paul.

Partial obedience is not obedience. Paul went to Troas, but the problems in Corinth overwhelmed him that he could not do what he was sent there to do—preach. God will never push us to do something we don't want to do. At times, we feel strong, we have faith and stand on the promises of God, but the cares of life can affect us deeply to walk away from where God is taking us.

He had no peace of mind. We, too, can get distracted by many things that happened yesterday that we lose focus on what is right in front of us. Delays can be frustrating, but God wants to give us His peace that transcends our understanding.

We are called to be proactive in our world. We cannot allow shifting circumstances to affect our emotions. We become defensive and reactive when we focus on the problems and the negative circumstances and lose sight of our priorities.

We can't give up before we even start. Instead, let us fix our gaze on God and the new thing He placed before us to touch and impact our surroundings.

Imagine

Oh, send out your light and your truth.
Let them lead me.

Psalm 43:3 (WEB)

Imagine waking up to get ready for the day and finding ourselves groping, trying to find our way as there is deep darkness in the room. We peek through the window, and there is nothing else but darkness. Imagine.

We think we're going through life a certain way, but circumstances happen; that hope and joy are gone, and suddenly, life has no luster. When everything around us seems bleak and gloomy, and we can't find our way, these are dark times in our souls.

As David said, "Why am I discouraged? Why is my heart so sad? I will put my hope in God! I will praise him again—my Savior and my God!" (Psalm 43:5, NLT).

David felt depressed and discouraged, but he also knew that there was hope in God. He did not allow that heaviness in his soul to pull him down. Instead, he reminded himself that God is greater and bigger than what he was going through. He did not want to give in to his feelings, and although the darkness was still around him, his attitude changed. That makes a whole lot of difference.

When we are struggling with many areas in our lives and are worried that everything is falling apart, and we don't know what our life is going to be, God knows. If we could only imagine the things that God has planned for us! God wants to bless us in a way we have not thought of. And if we don't have any strength left, we can learn from David to call on God. He comes to pull us out of that deep threatening darkness of the unknown and provide the light to our road to victory.

Even as we walk outside in the darkness, look up and see that vast display of the stars and experience the wonder of God's creativity and power. As written in Isaiah 40:26 (WEB),

> Lift up your eyes on high, and see who has created these who brings out their army by number. He calls them all by name. by the greatness of his might and because he is strong in power, not one is lacking.

God's light can break through the darkest times. His light is our reminder of His promises of love, healing, and forgiveness for a brighter tomorrow. As written, "The people who walk in darkness will see a great light. For those who live in a land of deep darkness, a light will shine" (Isaiah 9:2, NLT).

There may still be some dark times, but God's light brings such a contrast that as we walk in His light, a revelation that brings understanding and truth opens our minds to His faithfulness and love.

We each have something that no one else has, and the world is waiting. Discover the new meaning in your life and let that new you arise!

The Secret Place

The one who lives under the protection of the Most High dwells in the shadow of the Almighty.

Psalm 91:1 (HCSB)

Children love to create a secret place in their own magical world. Maybe, you imagine or wish you had such a secret place to enjoy and dream of the good life you've always wanted or to hide in times of chaos and trouble. It's not all wishful thinking.

God said, "'For I know the plans I have for you'—this is the Lord's declaration—'plans for your welfare, not for disaster, to give you a future and a hope'" (Jeremiah 29:11, HCSB). Did you ever notice that for every blessing and call of God over our lives, the enemy also tries to hinder or block us from advancing? Notice when we have a promise, suddenly, we are faced with financial problems, health issues, or relational situations. So, Psalm 91 talks about God's secret hiding place from the enemy, whose goal is to steal, kill, and destroy. God invites us to reside in that place with an incredible promise not only of protection but also of deliverance and victory over all powers of the enemy. How do we get into that secret place? It begins with Psalm 91:2 (KJV), "I will say of the Lord, 'He is my refuge and my fortress; My God, in Him I will trust.'"

The secret place is for those who have a relationship with God, having faith and trust to say with confidence, "You are my hiding place. You will preserve me from trouble. You will surround me with songs of deliverance. Selah" (Psalm 32:7, WEB). It's in that hiding place where we can separate ourselves from every distraction to hear the Lord's voice. He said, "I will instruct you and teach you in the way which you shall go. I will counsel you with my eye on you" (Psalm 32:8, WEB). Often, the biggest hindrance is us. We struggle to let go of being in control. When God wants to do a new thing, He will bring us back to that painful past to heal us. He will not only show us His goodness and faithfulness but also reveal incomprehensible and hidden things we may have never heard before.

In that secret place is His presence, and it does not matter where we are physically. We can be in our home, in the marketplace, traveling, among strangers, caught in a storm, yet He will hide us that even death cannot touch us. This is the promise.

The Autumn Leaves

*[...] casting all your worries on him,
because he cares for you.*

1 Peter 5:7 (WEB)

The view from my bedroom window stirred some nostalgic memories of the coming season and the promise of new things to come, new resolutions, and new beginnings. The majestic oak and the maple trees with leaves of blazing orange and deep golden yellows while the burning bush in flaming red—all speaking that a new season is here. It's hard to capture in words how autumn stirs the feelings in us. With a little breeze, a saffron leaf is floating down. An orange and an amber leaf gracefully flutter down like a swirl of many colors, like leaves dancing in the air, landing quietly on the green grass. And I wonder if the trees ever try to hold on to their beautiful leaves.

Nature shows us how they fully surrender to God. Do trees ever say, "I will keep my leaves this year and see how my next season goes?" I don't think so. Those trees, as designed, shed their leaves and never hold on to even one leaf. They let go of everything and get into the winter of rest until the new season of growth comes around.

Autumn signifies change. It brings the end of a season. The end of the long, hot summer days for shorter days and foggy, balmy to chilly darker nights. Time to pack away those crisp cotton clothes and put on some sweaters and fleece-lined boots. A perfect time to do some closet inventory and discard any clutter, old, unwanted, unnecessary garments. All this to say: Can you feel the change that's in the air? It is the season to let go.

Can we really let go of painful memories of our struggles or trauma? Joseph named his children to illustrate what God had done in his life. God made him forget the pain of his past through his firstborn. Then God made him fruitful through his second son. Joseph shifted into fruitfulness only after forgetting or letting go.

So, with us, though our summer is long and scorching, autumn with its chill in the air will surely come. We hover around that crackling fire for warmth, but we can learn how leaves gracefully let go of their grip on life. Let go of every leaf of anger, offense, unforgiveness, bitterness, disappointment, worry, and anxiety. We can declare that our dry and barren season is over and that we are entering a new season of fruitfulness.

Autumn is a time of harvest. But we cannot really be fruitful until we let go and forget the pain of the past. It's the season to examine what fruitfulness is being held back because we haven't forgotten something that we should have let go of. This is the kind of forgetfulness that brings a blessing.

God knows even the worst seasons of our lives. He can give us strength to let go so we can expect to receive that long-awaited breakthrough.

Seasons will surely come and go, but the love of God and His promises remain and never change.

About the Author

Marilyn Elshahawi originally came from the Philippines with one suitcase in her hand. After what seemed like an endless flight across the vast Pacific, stepping out on that beautiful spring day in New York, she realized she was in a whole new world. What followed seemed like a whirlwind of events when she got an unexpected short-term appointment at the United Nations and then met and married her Egyptian husband. What began as a brief visit to America changed her life forever. Out of one suitcase came an entire life. After a career of thirty-two years, having raised four children, she retires to then embark on a new venture: writing.

A Journey on the King's Road is Marilyn's first book. On typical days, as she spends time studying the Word of God, she is inspired to write her daily devotions. Marilyn's meticulous attention is given to language, period vernacular, translations, and, most importantly, contextual placement of scriptural words and events. Her unconventional approach is what captures her readers' attention, then captivates them to discover the truth in the life and times of some of the more obscure Bible characters. She brings to the forefront the peripheral perspective of the life and events of even well-known biblical characters who are so often categorically overlooked. It is her hope that readers from many generational walks and spiritual levels encounter a deeper revelation of the heart of the King.

When she's not writing at her favorite coffee shop or at home in New Jersey, where she lives with her husband, she spends time by the beach at their home in Florida.

CPSIA information can be obtained
at www.ICGtesting.com
Printed in the USA
BVHW051558030423
661670BV00004B/6